AF435936

First edition: May 2025
© Copyright of the work: Miguel Quemada
© Copyright of the edition: Angels Fortune Publishing Group
© Copyright of the translation: Miguel Quemada

Editing by Mª Isabel Montes Ramírez
ISBN: 979-13-990030-4-8
Digital ISBN: 979-13-990030-5-5
Editing and proofreading of the translation: Isabella Athanassiou
Layout and cover design: Cristina Lamata
Cover photo: Chimera depicted on a plate from Apulia (Italy) from the 4th century BC. Campana Collection, Louvre Museum, Paris. Photograph acquired by Miguel Quemada.

©Grupo Editorial Angels Fortune
www.angelsfortuneditions.com
info@angelsfortune.com

Barcelona (España)

CHIMERA

A patient's journey of hope
through transplantation

Miguel Quemada

For Cécile

Index

I

Prologue

The conclusion was undeniable: If I wanted to stay alive, I would have to become a chimera. I would also undergo periodic chimerism tests to ensure that the new state I had reached was stable. Doubtful, I signed the consent form despite being warned that I would have to go through a painful transformation process.

I left the office with uncertain steps and a puzzled mind. After much thought, I consulted a dictionary for the meaning of the word "chimera" to find out what future awaited me. It's striking how different the meanings of the word are; not all chimeras are the same, and each represents something different.

A Chimera is a mythological monster with very ancient origins, composed of the union of several animals. The classical myth describes a lion with a goat's head growing from its back and another head of a serpent on its tail. It breathes fire, and its representations show not a beautiful or attractive animal but rather a terrible and unsympathetic monster that ravages the earth's surface whenever it ascends from its lair in the depths of the earth.

Chimeras are also a product of the imagination. They are passions that are longed for or pursued even though they may not be possible. To be generous, we can think of them as having a positive side, since most chimeras are youthful daydreams that we pursue naively or with good intentions, even if they cannot become reality. The word itself still carries a certain negative connotation because, as unreachable illusions, they can lead to frustration or cause people to abandon more realistic goals, driving them away from rational analysis.

In biology, a chimera is a living being resulting from the union of genetically distinct cells from different organisms. In the past, chimeras in higher animals were not viable, but modern medicine has managed to develop them through transplants and keep them alive with treatments. A person who has received an organ transplant has become a "human chimera" because their body is composed of cells with different genetic compositions. They will remain a chimera for the rest of their life, and although there may be rejection between the receiving body and the donated organ, these can be medically controlled to ensure coexistence.

Among these forms of chimerism, there is a particular case: that of bone marrow transplants. These are performed to cure blood or lymphatic system diseases. The patient's dysfunctional bone marrow is destroyed, and the new stem cells implanted from the donor will give rise to new bone marrow. This bone marrow takes root in the bones and begins to produce blood, spreading throughout the body. The patient changes blood type and adopts the donor's, becoming a chimera with cells of both genetic compositions: Those of the new blood and those of the original body. This is a true rebirth, achieved after a traumatic treatment. The feeling of being reborn is reinforced during recovery, when it is necessary to repeat the childhood vaccination schedule, as the immune system's memory is lost with the replacement of the bone marrow.

In my case, the donor was my sister. The chimera I accepted to become harbors my new XX chromosomal bone marrow alongside the rest of my cells, which are XY. The blood generated by my new bone marrow is also XX. The periodic chimerism tests I undergo consist of checking that my blood is feminine. As long as it is, the transplant is stable; if masculine cells appear in my blood, it indicates a problem, immediate hospital admission.

I am proud to say that now "feminism runs in my blood." On the other hand, the idea of the "chimeric beast," representing destruction and ancient depths, both imposes respect and fills me with dread. That is why I write this novel, to discover who I have become and to make sense of this monstrous chimera, which at the same time can be the embodiment of youthful dreams.

The theft of the black pearls

It all began with a phone call. It was Saturday afternoon, and some jewelry had disappeared from the luxurious home of a respectable family in Madrid. The previous night, a dinner party had been held with six guests joining the owners of the house. As on other occasions, after dinner, the guests moved to the living room, where they had a drink surrounded by some of the finest art the family owned.

At the far end of the room, covering an entire wall, hung an excellent painting by Tàpies. On the side walls, prominent engravings by Picasso and Miró were displayed, and on a ledge between the windows were two exquisite small Flemish oil paintings from the early Renaissance. In one of the corners, a glass case housed about a dozen large, smooth black pearls, which, placed on a green velvet cushion, could easily go unnoticed on a first visit. There were many other jewelry pieces of goldwork displayed on the shelves around the room, but the stolen items, taken after breaking the case, were the black pearls.

Among the guests was the owners' son, accompanied by his new girlfriend, an American woman with a calm smile and an intelligent gaze. They had met at a party hosted by the American company he worked for, where she was doing a professional internship. What initially seemed like a brief romance had already lasted over six months, leading him to introduce her to his parents. She was very attractive—tall like her boyfriend and of athletic build, with a determined air she seemed to want to conceal. A New Yorker by origin, she spoke grammatically perfect Spanish with a slight, almost imperceptible Anglo-Saxon accent.

Another guest was a Colombian businessman, accompanied by his wife, who was also very beautiful and from the same country. He was involved in maritime trade, although I couldn't specify much more about his work despite receiving a detailed description of what he did. In summary, it was about the buying and selling of various goods, and he managed the ships and containers that transported them. It was a complex job, highly exposed to geopolitical conditions, requiring his full dedication as well as that of his employees and collaborators in his Swiss office. He traveled frequently between America and Europe, and had recently acquired an apartment in Madrid's Salamanca neighborhood to have a base in the city. He often used nautical terms in his vocabulary—"base of operations," "ports of destination," "crew"—and if he occasionally let slip a term from the jargon of other businesses, like "wheeling and dealing" or "speculating," he would immediately correct himself without giving it much importance. He had planned to fly to Bogotá on Sunday night but had postponed it to the following week at the request of the police investigating the case.

The dinner party was completed by a couple of well-preserved men in their fifties with an elegant appearance. They were married and had been friends of the hosts for many years. One of them, the younger one, worked in the fashion world, while the other, who sported perfectly manicured nails, was involved in the art market. They owned a gallery near Alonso Martínez, descending toward Chueca, where they exhibited works by national and international contemporary artists. The older man was dressed elegantly but casually, and it was clear that he took great care of his physical appearance. He was the more dominant of the two and told me that most of their clients who purchased art came from Salamanca or from private residences in the Madrid area, such as those in La Moraleja, with whose owners they had had long-standing relationships. The information about the clients was strictly confidential, and he could only tell me that they sold visual art—paintings and sculptures, mainly—but also various types of design and combinations that could be described as "indefinable." His partner, though only four or five years younger, had a youthful face, spoke little, and smiled a lot. When I interviewed them for the first time, they came to my office together, and I had to insist on speaking with them separately as I needed independent accounts.

Following the police investigations, I was allowed to interview each of the dinner guests. I obtained statements from all of them in the days following the theft, and, for better or worse, contradictions began to surface that I won't dwell on here. That night, only the homeowners had slept in the house. Almost all of the others had left around midnight, with the son and his girlfriend staying about half an hour longer to chat with the parents.

The pearls were shown to me only in a photograph taken at the pedestal where they had been displayed until the theft. Although large for their species, they could easily fit into a fist and could have been hidden together or separately to smuggle them out of the house. At the crime scene, there were shards from the protective glass case, which had been broken with a sharp object. An irregular opening allowed a hand to pass through the glass, leaving little doubt about the method used in the theft. Whoever had done it didn't seem to be a professional, but they were careful and skilled enough to accomplish it. There were traces of a putty applied to control the breakage, which was fairly clean except near the side closest to the living room, where there were some imperfections in the hole. No fingerprints or traces of tools were left—only one misstep that could lead to the thief's downfall: A shard of glass had lightly scratched the skin, leaving a small trace of what appeared to be blood. Forensic scientists took a sample, which they sent to the hematology lab. We had the analysis results within a week.

A mistaken interpretation of the evidence is a sure-fire path to error. The only available vaccine is distrust. Suspicion of the evidence, because it motivates us to verify and cross-check it. Doubt of oneself, because it keeps us away from presumption and gullibility. If I had followed these simple premises, I would still be working as a private detective. However, there are occasions when letting mistakes carry us away can bring satisfactions that we can only appreciate in hindsight.

The insurance company had hired me to find the culprit, but from the beginning, I was warned that the pearls were only insured for ten thousand euros, a trivial sum compared to the ten million euros covering the rest of the collection. We were to provide excellent service, as this was an important client, but the theft itself was considered minor. Apart from my financial interest—I earned better fees when the stolen items were of high value—I couldn't help but wonder why, among other items with higher monetary value, the black pearls were the ones stolen. There were obvious reasons: Their size made them easy to hide and transport, and with the right contacts, they could be sold quickly and profitably. However, other pieces in the collection, like some gold items inlaid with diamonds, were insured for larger amounts and weren't taken. The Flemish paintings were the size of a laptop and could have been stolen without much difficulty. As for their resale price, I wouldn't dare to estimate, but it was likely to have several zeros attached to it. Unless I was mistaken, the thief had entered with a specific target in mind: the black pearls.

That weekend, a housekeeper had also stayed in the residence. She had served dinner on Saturday and was the first to notice the theft while cleaning the living room the next morning. Upon seeing the broken glass around the pedestal, she stopped and immediately informed the homeowners, aware that a crime had taken place.

That Saturday morning, two workers had also begun the regular maintenance of the garden, which was done periodically. The maintenance included trimming the lawn, cutting branches that were too close to the house's windows, and general care of the bushes, which were already displaying their first spring flowers. They started their work near the stone parapet below the glassed-in living room, which could have given them access to the pearls, facilitating the theft. There was enough noise and tools to serve as a cover for a well-planned theft.

After interviewing the guests and workers, all of them seemed suspicious to me. I ruled out the lady of the house, though, because I was so captivated by her presence—beautiful and elegant like a modern-day Nefertiti—that I couldn't imagine her being responsible for any wrongdoing. We had to wait for the results of the few pieces of available evidence to advance the investigation. The chromosomal analysis of the blood was conclusive: The perpetrator was a man, reducing the number of suspects to seven. We took blood samples from the seven individuals and sent them for detailed genetic analysis. After nearly five weeks, and after comparing the samples, we concluded that none of them matched.

Nevertheless, there was still the possibility that they had hired a thief to do the dirty work during the dinner. This way, the instigator's involvement could have been limited to leaving a window open or somehow providing access to the thief. In short, although it initially seemed that the available evidence would make the case easy to solve, after cross-referencing it, we hadn't moved far from the starting point.

I focused my efforts on figuring out how the thief might have entered the house. I found no traces or evidence supporting the theory of an external intruder. The windows, sealed tightly, hadn't been forced; the alarm system, reinforced at the potential entry points to the living room housing the artwork, showed no signs of detecting any intruder. The two cameras monitoring the exterior of the living room's windows only recorded the gardeners doing their work in the morning and a small fox taking a nocturnal stroll along the flower bed surrounding the house.

Two things were clear to me: No one had entered unseen to commit the theft, and none of the people present at the time were suitable suspects.

By now, the police were losing interest in the case, and I was so stuck that I began thinking about other weak links in the investigation that might open up a new path forward. From the beginning, something hadn't added up. Those pearls were hiding something, perhaps a clue I couldn't decipher. I reached out to a trusted jeweler to see if he could deduce anything from the photographs of the stolen pieces. To my surprise, as soon as he saw them, his interest was piqued, but he told me that before recounting an intriguing story, it would be best to know if any of the pearls had remained in the house.

The homeowners didn't seem happy when I relayed the jeweler's question. At first, they tried to evade it, but eventually, they showed me a family heirloom: a gold brooch with one of the pearls set as a pendant, like a teardrop. They kept it in the safe with the rest of their personal jewelry, and despite its striking appearance—or perhaps precisely because it was so conspicuous—they couldn't recall the last time the lady of the house had worn it.

When the jeweler saw the pearl, he didn't hesitate for a moment: Black pearls of that style were very rare and of excellent quality, found mostly in Madrid and Barcelona. They came from families who had fled the Philippines at the end of the colonial period. The more cautious families had sold their possessions and exchanged everything they had accumulated for those valuable, exquisite pearls, which were easy to transport. They used the pearls to start new lives wherever they went. Upon arriving in Spain, they sold them little by little. On one hand, they provided substantial income every time they parted with one, but on the other, they were a reminder of better times and a symbol of nobility for a few families. Over time, those pearls had become legendary in the world of jewelry, easily recognizable. Today, they were highly sought after, and when one appeared, it was immediately bought for sums that could be exorbitant, depending on the size and purity of the pearl.

If the photograph didn't lie, and having seen one of the originals, selling these pearls for a considerable amount would be very easy in discreet markets for anyone with even minimal contacts.

I told the jeweler the amount for which the pearls were insured. He smiled—"That wouldn't even cover one night's rent." I asked if he could think of any reason why they would have been insured for such a low amount. "You're the one working for an insurance company," he replied, "so you know better than I do why some valuable properties are insured for less than their worth or, in some cases, aren't insured at all." This confirmed my suspicions: The origins of those pearls were tied to something shameful, or perhaps scandalous—something secret that no one wanted to publicize. They might have been stolen, even as part of an arranged theft, or acquired in a dubious auction, or they could have ended up in the current owners' hands after a dishonorable plunder. Many valuable artworks and jewels came from Nazi looting of Jewish families during World War II. Their current owners often opt not to publicize this and prefer to enjoy the pieces or their possession discreetly, always keeping them safe and secure. Clearly, a new line of investigation was opening up—a good thread to start pulling to unravel the mystery.

However, the homeowners were not going to be much help. The pearls had been passed down through the husband's family, including the brooch with the teardrop-shaped pearl, which had belonged to his grandmother, though he couldn't remember seeing her wear it. They didn't have any paperwork proving the origin of the pearls, nor did they know where they had been acquired—or at least that's the version they told me.

I asked the police, but they had already completely lost interest in the case: Jewels of similar value disappeared in Madrid by the hundreds every day, without violence or victims, and this case had been shelved as a minor one. They had issued alerts to different police stations in case similar pearls were found among the loot occasionally recovered, and if any suspicious pieces appeared, they would notify the homeowners to come and inspect them in the reserved display. The dinner guests had been allowed to leave the country, and both the housekeeper and the gardeners, who had been temporarily suspended from their duties, had resumed their work as usual. A month later, it seemed as though nothing had happened in that house—it was as if there had been no theftat all. What's more, my unsuccessful attempts to pursue new lines of investigation were no longer welcome, and the homeowners were just waiting to collect the insurance payout and forget about the case.

In these circumstances, I heard something surprising from colleagues in my field: The head of the house had hired a private detective to discreetly investigate the whereabouts of the stolen pearls. Two obvious points: The hired detective wasn't me, and the homeowner knew the real value of those jewels.

I had a hunch that investigating more about the other suspects could help me understand the mystery better. As I mentioned earlier, they all seemed guilty to me, but I won't go into detail on what I found out about each of them or how much time I wasted doing it. Suffice it to say, I followed the wrong order, which delayed me significantly.

The Colombian and his wife fit all the clichés of being the masterminds of the theft, and like a rookie, I let myself be carried away by my prejudices, so they were the first ones I interviewed. It was hard to get information about their activities, and a review of their history suggested it would be easy to include a jewel theft with subsequent sale on the black market. However, I found no evidence that they had been involved in the disappearance of the pearls.

The gay couple, at first glance, had much more respectable backgrounds. Digging a bit into their businesses, I discovered some shady dealings in the sale of paintings, probably aimed at laundering money through dubious invoices. The amounts weren't large, but they showed a certain skill in shady matters and an appetite for easy money. Who knows if, given the chance to increase profits, they might have applied their expertise to something bigger.

Finally, I turned my attention to investigating the son of the owner and his girlfriend—or rather, ex-girlfriend, since the couple had broken up a week after the dinner and she had returned to New York. The man seemed very affected by the breakup, on the verge of depression. He knew nothing about the theft of the pearls and wasn't interested in the slightest. At first, I thought he might be acting, but I soon realized his distress was genuine, and

I ruled him out as a suspect. Among his disjointed statements, he revealed one thing that changed the course of the investigation: One of the plans he had canceled was a trip to Manila to attend the opening of some old warehouses by the port, recently restored and incorporated into the city's tourist circuit. The warehouses had belonged to the maternal ancestors of his ex-girlfriend and still bore the surname of a distinguished colonial family, now almost forgotten in the Anglo-Saxon side of the family. I'm someone who believes that coincidences don't exist, so a trip to New York was in order.

The insurance company didn't share my opinion; they considered the case closed and were ready to pay the indemnity to the insured parties. They hinted that during the vacation I was about to take, I could take the opportunity to visit the city on my own, and they told me I could take my time returning since they didn't need me for the moment. They also requested that I stop bothering the owners, as they had received complaints about my insistence.

With these avenues of investigation closed, I decided to send an exploratory email to Julia, the ex-girlfriend, who was friendly and willing to meet with me. She was very busy at the moment but said she would have some time in about four weeks. If that was acceptable to me, I could contact her then to arrange a meeting. I didn't mind the plan; it gave me time to wrap up a few pending issues in Madrid and to buy a plane ticket at a reasonable price. Considering how dark my job prospects were becoming, I wasn't in a position to splurge. Meanwhile, I had a few weeks to gather information about Julia's maternal family history. I already knew the illustrious surname, and the dates were sufficiently narrowed down.

When they returned from the Philippines, they settled in Barcelona and opened a grocery store on Balmes Street. As Julia later confirmed during our interview, the acquisition of the store and one of the apartments they used as their residence was thanks to the sale of the first pearls. The pearls also helped finance a good education for the younger family members and allowed them to integrate with the Catalan bourgeoisie.

One of the newly immigrated sons, her great-grandfather, was a good student and graduated in law before the end of the Great War in Europe. He began working as a lawyer, but he had political inclinations and a great talent for business. After a few years, he decided to move to Madrid with his wife and four children. The 1920s were glorious for him too. He founded several companies and amassed a large fortune, frequently traveling to France and England, specializing in international trade. At the same time, he retained his concern for the country's development and progress. He was a liberal with a broad vision for the future, convinced that education was key to social prosperity. He was involved in the Ateneo and attended as many conferences as he could, soon mingling with the cultural elites of the capital. He collaborated with the Free Institution of Education, helping to acquire land and set up new schools. He navigated the 1929 economic crisis with some skill, and by the 1930s, he had accumulated considerable wealth, much of it secured through real estate acquisitions. Steering clear of extremism, he sided with the Republic when the Spanish Civil War broke out. Although his finances took a hard hit during the war, he did his best to help friends and support the Republican legitimate government financially. The family's experience during the war was disastrous; only his wife and one of his daughters survived. Economically, the postwar period was equally devastating. As relatives of a significant Republican figure, they lost all their possessions except for an apartment on María de Molina Street, where the two survivors settled.

When I met with Julia, I was certain I was speaking to the granddaughter of that child who lived on María de Molina Street. However, I still needed to fill in the gaps in the more recent history. Julia herself told me that, to survive in the decades following the war, her great-grandmother took in female students from Wellesley College who were staying in Madrid. She had the necessary American contacts from before the war, and her good reputation allowed her to secure essential income to survive those years. Additionally, when Julia's grandmother reached university age, she was able to get a scholarship to study at Wellesley, something that would have been highly improbable in her hometown. Julia's eyes lit up when she talked about her grandmother. Married to a prestigious American professor, she had started the family genealogy across the Atlantic. Although she was fully integrated into her adopted country, she had passed on the language and family legends to her descendants.

The net was closing in on Julia. She was unaware of it, but the pieces I was collecting from different sources were fitting together, revealing the final image of the puzzle. I was sure the pearls had belonged to her maternal family and that she had returned after many years to recover them. However, I still couldn't figure out how she had done it. In any case, I would find out. I would solve the case and return with honor to my position as a detective at the insurance company.

For now, I organized close surveillance. Since she considered herself free of suspicion, it would be easy to track her movements and habits—naivety leaves us unarmed. I spent several days following her, learning interesting things about her, such as where she lived, worked, and whom she visited. Nothing relevant to the case in those initial days of surveillance—just getting myself familiar with the scene.

A little over a week had passed when I began to uncover relevant information that would soon accelerate events. One sunny morning, she left her workplace, took the subway to the eastern part of the city near the medical campuses, bought a coffee and something to eat from a small stand by Santa Caterina Park, then sat on an outdoor bench. She took a book from her bag and began to read, though she seemed restless and had difficulty concentrating, frequently glancing at her watch. Finally, she stood up, crossed the first avenue and headed toward the river down 67th Street. She stopped halfway down the block and entered the Memorial Sloan Kettering Cancer Center with a hesitant step.

I followed her inside, feeling as though I were intruding upon her private life, and waited at a safe distance near the entry checkpoint. She was greeted warmly, as if a regular visitor, but still had to identify herself and mention the doctor she was there to see. Once she had passed the checkpoint, I attempted to follow, using the excuse of visiting a relative. It was futile; privacy was strictly upheld, and even asking questions raised suspicion. I had a chance to glance over the desk and confirm that Julia's name had been listed among the patients, not the visitors.

I went outside and waited, using my phone to search for information about the doctor she was visiting. He specialized in bone marrow transplants—or more accurately, in blood stem cell transplants—and mainly performed patient follow-ups at this hospital. Julia emerged after half an hour, smiling and walking with newfound confidence. She headed east, and upon reaching Caspary Auditorium, glanced around as if looking for someone. A tall, handsome young man, strikingly similar to her, rose from a bench. They exchanged a kiss on the cheek and, after a few quiet words, embraced. She closed her eyes in the hug, and I thought I saw a single tear slip down her cheek. They walked into the concert hall together, side by side, exchanging brief glances with shared smiles.

I sat off to the side, in a spot where I could see her from a diagonal angle. As a piano and violin duo performed works by Albéniz, I admired her delicate profile. Slender, with sharp features, she listened to the music with a serene, calm smile, as if she had been waiting a long time for this moment, as if she had just received good news that had been long overdue.

By this point, I had learned she had been on medical leave for an entire year and could assume that her doctor's visit was for the periodic control of a bone marrow transplant. She had most likely received it over two years ago and had been given good news at her annual check-up. The transplant could have come from a close relative, possibly her younger brother, the man who attended the concert with her. If that was the case, that woman had male blood, with an XY chromosomal composition. Perhaps the insignificant trace of blood—the only revealing clue—found on a shard of glass from the urn that had contained the pearls was not a coincidence. Perhaps the thief had left it there on purpose, so our investigation would focus solely on male suspects. Or maybe these were just my speculations, serving to help me find answers in this obsessive case that was driving me mad and leading me to ruin. Still, the hypothesis wasn't entirely far-fetched, and if it was true, Julia had managed to evade suspicion long enough to leave Spain and secure the stolen pearls.

The next step in the investigation was to obtain a sample of her blood and compare it genetically with the blood found on the urn—a complicated task. Practically speaking, I could start with a saliva sample or something similar. If the transplant had been from her brother, the analysis would show a high similarity to the blood on the urn, and that would be enough to convince a judge to order a blood sample from Julia for a definitive comparison.

With the hope of making progress along this line, I arranged a second meeting with Julia. She was glad to know that I still had a week left in New York, and she made an appointment with me for the next Friday. We agreed to meet for a drink in the afternoon, but she would have to leave afterward, as she had plans to attend a ceremony that might be of interest to me. I accepted the afternoon meeting, but I couldn't attend the ceremony, as my flight back was early on Saturday morning. I had a few days left to find out where the pearls had gone and gather more information before our meeting.

A few days earlier, I had asked a good friend and fellow detective to investigate if there had been any transactions regarding this matter in the black market, from Antwerp to Los Angeles. It wasn't that complicated; at a Sotheby's auction held on York Avenue, just over six million dollars had been paid for a dozen black pearls about a month ago. I was able to review the catalog and confirm that they were the ones I was looking for, but it was impossible to obtain information about the seller or the buyer, their origin, or destination. At least, we had found them, and we had proof that they had crossed the Atlantic—another piece of the puzzle that pointed to Julia as the perpetrator of the crime.

I spoke again with the insurance company, convinced that I could persuade them that it was worth continuing the investigation. I was wrong; first, they doubted that the same jewels insured for ten thousand euros were the ones sold at Sotheby's, and second, they reminded me that the case was closed: They had paid the compensation and had no intention of reopening it. Finally, they told me that, in case I hadn't understood in the previous conversation, my contract had ended. They didn't yet drop the fatal word "fired"; they reserved it for the conversation we had, amid veiled threats, early the next morning.

Meanwhile, I decided to take what I saw as the most logical route: I phoned the owner of the pearls, hoping he might be interested in the auction result. He answered curtly, telling me I was getting involved in something that was none of my business and that I was overstepping my bounds. It's no surprise that, between one thing and another, they opened the door for me—or perhaps I pushed it open myself.

At the café where we had arranged to meet, I had to wait only a couple of minutes; shortly after I sat down, Julia walked in. Attractive, elegant—there are women who know how to show their beauty as if they were disguising it. I had barely asked any questions when she began to talk about her Spanish family, confirming what I had found out. She told me that her great-grandfather died sick at the end of the siege of Madrid, but still, once the war was over, he was given a fine, which had to be paid. To do so, all the real estate properties were sold off, except for the apartment that her grandmother kept to live with her mother. A supposed family friend, sympathetic to the regime, acted as an intermediary in all the operations, and since more funds were still needed to pay the fine, he appropriated the family jewels, eyed long before, for a measly sum of money.

The black pearls brought from the Philippines held a prominent place in the collection and also in the legends her grandmother told. They had always accompanied the family, used as wedding arras, and were a symbol of an aristocratic past. Probably, the supposed friend of her father thought that by taking the pearls, he was also appropriating the glorious past that accompanied them, but the only thing he took with him was the ignominy of plundering and the shame of betraying a companion. "With friends like that," her grandmother used to say. In any case, they were never a source of pride, but a symbol of disgrace. She displayed them in a reserved corner of her house, as if they were a stain waiting to be erased by time. Their bequeathal to her descendants was very discreet, and the pearls fell out of favor.

At this point, I let out a smile—it was now that Julia was going to tell me that she had stolen them from their current owners to "relieve them of a burden." However, her confession would have to wait. She apologized for answering a phone call she was receiving at that moment, got up, and went outside to take it.

I stayed at the table, going over what she had told me. I had already met several families who were victims of Francoist plundering, but Julia's tenacity was impressive. It was hard to know if she had done it to recover the money she considered hers or if she pursued higher principles of justice. Given her determination, I leaned toward the second option, also influenced by the sympathy this woman awakened in me, although my job prevents me from indulging in such weaknesses, as they bring us too close to the suspects. In this case, I could even speak of a "culprit," though she had yet to reveal her responsibility in the theft. From my table, I could see her through the window, talking on the phone, looking across the street, her back to me, so I took the opportunity to collect in a handkerchief the glass from which Julia had drunk. I had the sample I needed, enough for a genetic analysis, the first step to unmasking this elusive chimera.

When she sat down again, she asked me if I had enjoyed the concert the other day. "It's a theater with formidable acoustics, especially for chamber music," she observed. I merely replied that discretion was part of my job and that although I had considered bumping into her during the intermission, I held back when I saw she was with someone. "That's my younger brother," she said, "If you had come over to greet me, I would have introduced you to him." Her words gradually confirmed my suspicions to the point that I wanted to hint that she shouldn't keep tightening the noose around herself. However, it already felt like a farewell. She was going to the ceremony she had invited me to, and I couldn't attend—what a shame, because perhaps there I would have found answers to some of the questions that kept haunting me. Before she left, she handed me a periodical from the cancer association and assured me that in it, I could find information about the ceremony that might be of interest to me.

I stayed a while longer in the café, browsing through the magazine she had left me. She had marked a double-page spread that compiled information on the annual donations, highlighting an anonymous one of six million euros received recently, destined to fund leukemia research. The donation included an express wish to create a pre-treatment center for childhood cancer in Manila and a bone marrow bank in the Philippines.

I suppose that was the closest I was going to get to a confession of guilt. I had reached the end of the road, following a path previously drawn by Julia, both in her steps and in time. This time, I was completely disarmed. As I said at the beginning, there are times when being led by one's own mistakes shapes the course of life, and it's only when we look back that we can appreciate it.

It was nightfall, and it was cold. I walked indifferently toward the avenue where I would find a taxi back to my hotel. Before turning the corner, I took the water glass with the saliva sample I still had in my coat pocket and tossed it into a recycling bin.

II

The Chimera

The chimera, as a mythological creature, horrifies me. I've tried to find some appealing depictions to feel captivated by them, but they are all monstrous. The most common representations are those with three heads emerging from a hybrid body. Even the heads of the animals—lion, goat, and serpent in their most common form—convey tension and violence. In large part because they are usually shown breathing fire from all three mouths, displaying both their origin and their destructive power.

The most frequent depictions are found in Greek pottery and some Roman mosaics, many showing the death of the Chimera at the hands of Bellerophon. There is an Etruscan bronze on display at the Archaeological Museum of Florence that embodies the monster in all its splendor. Although of unquestionable beauty, what it transmits is fear.

The Chimera is an ancient, mythical creature that was born in the depths of the earth and formed from irrational and mysterious forces, giving rise to a dark being with a home in the underworld. Occasionally, it would emerge to the surface and destroy everything in its path, spewing fire and leaving behind a desolate, scorched landscape. Legends say it was located in Asia Minor, where it was feared.

After all that has been said, it's no surprise that the idea of becoming a chimera gives me an initial feeling of revulsion. From an optimistic perspective, improving the behavior of my predecessors should be quite easy. On the other hand, it was inspiring to find some examples of more suggestive chimeras, and the one depicted on a Greek ceramic plate from Apulia, displayed in the Louvre Museum, was a good way to start. I continued digging through various scholarly and artistic interpretations, and I managed to discover something positive.

This is not the case with Paul Diel[1], who, in studying Greek symbols, presents the chimera as imaginative exaltation that can only be overcome by man if dominated by spiritual energy, represented by Pegasus. This would be a version of the passion-versus-reason dichotomy. In this interpretation, the lion represents the perversion of material desires, the goat represents sexual appetite, and the dragon or serpent symbolizes deceit. Pegasus, the winged horse gifted by Athena, which Bellerophon rode to slay the Chimera, represents reason and spirituality capable of overcoming perversions. It's a very black-and-white view in which the mythological monster gets the short end of the stick.

For Robert Graves[2], the Chimera is a very ancient calendar symbol, already found in the temples of the Hittites in Asia Minor. The lion represents spring, the goat represents summer, and the dragon or serpent represents winter. The entire chimera is an allegory of time and the passing of life, associated with primitive matriarchal societies that were later dominated by the

Greeks. Therefore, some of that force, associated with mysterious and deep nature, was incorporated into classical mythology as an Oriental-origin myth with an esoteric character. Its destructive nature was evident when it breathed fire, and though it commands the respect of ancient things, its annihilation by Bellerophon relegates it to another era, not opening the door to the rational Greek world. Again, it's difficult to find a positive reading in this interpretation.

Poets, however, have managed to provide more attractive images. In *La desolación de la Quimera* ("Desolation of the Chimera"[3]) by Luis Cernuda, when the Chimera whispers to the moon, it does so in a sweet voice, a voice that soothes its desolation. From this horrible, decadent monster, an extremely tender voice emanates to lament the path humanity has chosen. Men have distanced themselves from the Chimera, from those hidden, subterranean forces that once attracted them, which, though they could drag them into madness, also made them capable of dreams, love, and ambitious works of art. Cernuda reinterprets the monster's role in a more generous way. The hidden and imaginative forces it represents are also creative, capable of generating a vigorous world rooted in the most instinctual nature of humanity. It is that primal, original world that many artists have sought as the foundation for their work, even if it meant sacrificing their lives to peer into the abyss of madness. Thus, the poem offers a positive vision of the monster's symbolism.

If we apply this concept to human beings, the Chimera could represent the subconscious, even the unconscious, which we rarely confront and which holds hidden keys that could explain our existence. Among the most famous chimeras of this type are those of Gérard de Nerval, a prominent poet of French Romanticism. He suffered from fits of madness from his youth and even embraced them as moments when he could dive into his deepest imaginary world to enrich his creative capacity. Not surprisingly, several of his most personal works originated during these periods of madness, such as the esoteric sonnets, difficult to interpret, which he grouped under the name *Les Chimères* ("The Chimeras"[4]). Understanding this journey into the depths of human nature and madness is quite the challenge, but no one can deny the influence he had on many writers afterward, and the fascination his character and tragic death held for later avant-garde movements like Surrealism.

So, the Chimera is gradually taking shape as a primal source of creativity, difficult to tame but undeniably rich. It is the abyss into which Munch, Van Gogh, or Chagall gazed to fuel their paintings. It is the endless labyrinth where humans move blindly, stumbling, always uncertain of advancing. For the matter of concern, it's enough to say that this monstrous Chimera reveals favorable aspects that initially seemed rejected.

In today's rational world, the Chimera remains a refuge symbolizing primal and imaginative forces. Its visual representation has softened a bit throughout history, and chimeras now no longer only include the three-headed hybrid beast seen in the earliest images. In later versions of classical mythology, it is an animal composed of two realities, giving way to sirens, centaurs, griffins, and other imaginary beings that can be suggestive or even captivating.

But let's not be overly optimistic. A chimera is not the same as a crucible. The two words may seem similar in meaning, but there is a subtle difference, and we all know that the devil is in the details. Figuratively speaking, a crucible refers to a reality composed of the fusion of several others. It is very common to use this term for a society or territory where communities with different origins, beliefs, or traditions have lived together harmoniously. The connotations of the word are clearly positive and evoke respect and tolerance as the key values that enrich the whole. Toledo, as a crucible of cultures, gave rise to the School of Translators, a forerunner of modern universities, allowing interaction among Jews, Arabs, and Christians for the exchange of knowledge and texts. Arab-Norman art reflects the crucible of styles in Sicily, where the blending of different artistic traditions produced an explosion of beauty. In summary, a crucible highlights the positive aspects of mixtures, while chimeras carry within their diversity the seeds of destruction.

Let's leave that chimerical realm of mysterious meaning for poets and artists and adapt the meaning to the new chimeras we are becoming. We are a sum of realities, as medicine tells us, but of deep realities that affect our most intimate and uncontrollable selves. Perhaps the most remarkable thing is that in the process of creating these chimeras, we've had to face the abyss of pain, the fear of organ rejection, the sense of being completely vulnerable, and the knowledge that our life hangs by a thread beyond our control.

All of this offers us the opportunity to become people with a renewed ability to value life and those around us. Just as the artist who peers into madness gains the ability to create the most beautiful works of humanity, the new chimeras, who have felt the thin ice of the frozen lake beneath our feet, can rise again with a renewed vital humanism.

The artist's reencounter

Every morning, Antonio would wake up early and listen to the news on the radio—economy, politics, international affairs—while he got ready. During breakfast, he would check the invitations to the week's events, scheduling them into his phone. At the same time, he would read the messages he had received overnight from family and friends living in different time zones. There were so many notifications and communications that, on some days, he would leave the table without even finishing his coffee, sometimes drinking it without even paying attention. In fact, he couldn't remember the last time he had sat down and enjoyed a good breakfast without thinking about anything else.

He took the metro near his house, and during the ride to work, he updated his social media accounts. Not too many—one for neighbors, another for parents at his child's daycare, and the rest related to his job or hobbies. He quickly skimmed through the first two, without paying much attention to the messages. He read the work and hobby-related ones more carefully in case there was anything important or of interest. Even so, it wasn't unusual for him to be reading the messages in bits and pieces, on the platform or even while walking on the sidewalk to his destination, just to have them reviewed before the day's classes began.

He taught Art History and Technical Drawing at a high school in central Madrid. His students were between 14 and 16 years old—a heterogeneous group despite the uniformity of that age when personalities have yet to fully develop. Some had a natural talent for drawing and painting, showing a lot of interest in class—the kind of advanced students who lift the teacher's spirits. Then there were others, less gifted in the visual arts, or perhaps in any art at all, who struggled just to avoid failing. Overall, he didn't have many complaints about his students. They were good kids who appreciated his efforts to make lessons engaging and informative. Some days, of course, were more challenging: Students would be rowdy, or a small group would decide to disrupt the class, but when Antonio reflected at the end of each term, the balance always tipped in favor of the positive side.

His job didn't excite him, but he found it appealing enough, and it provided a good career that brought him security. He enjoyed combining the creativity of preparing lessons with the pedagogy of engaging with his students. However, after six years, he couldn't help but feel the job becoming routine. Not in the sense that each day was exactly the same as the previous one, but that habit had dulled his excitement for the things that happened or their potential to captivate him. He identified the most talented students and encouraged them to hone their skills, practice, and improve. Most of them did, improving significantly. However, none of them painted any exceptional work that would have made a real impact. While he continued to teach, he had lost the hope of discovering a student with a true artistic calling. That's not to say that none of his students would ever become an artist; rather, he had come to accept that he wouldn't be the one to teach a genuine painter.

Antonio had started painting as a child, and by the age of 14, he had already discovered his vocation. Wherever he went—sitting on a terrace or facing a landscape—he would draw in a small sketchbook he always carried with him. He did it for fun, just as some of his peers played instruments in local bands or sang in the choir. He took drawing and painting classes from a teacher who recognized his talent and encouraged him to continue. Once he mastered the technique of still life in the studio, she took him to paint landscapes in the open air and to museums to copy the masters.

It was in late adolescence that his artistic vocation turned into a passion. He began to discover the aesthetic ambition in the works of other painters, starting with the classic Spanish, Italian, and Flemish artists, and later moving on to the modern and contemporary ones. Soon, he became captivated by the search for beauty, for a way to represent both the world around him and the emotions it stirred within him. Copying and repeating learned techniques was no longer enough for him; he needed to develop a personal style that set him apart from the rest, a way to show his point of view and discover new forms of expressing reality. The ultimate freedom was in exploring shapes and colors, finding the original combination on a canvas that led to the perfect expression. In short, Antonio felt the Chimera breathing down his neck, and the only thing that mattered to him was art—contributing directly to the capital-H History of Art.

When he enrolled in the Faculty of Fine Arts, he was already deeply fascinated by the avant-garde movements of the early 20th century. If he could have lived out a dream, it would have been to experience the bohemian life in Paris, Vienna, or Berlin. Paris, more than anywhere else, seemed the perfect place—to have mingled with the Cubists or debated with the Surrealists was his idea of the ultimate pleasure. Letting go of everyday constraints, small economies, and routines to fully immerse himself in discussing modes of expression between sips of wine and absinthe—what a wonderful way to live! To lose oneself among oils and brushes, surrounded by canvases and boards, abandoning life's routine obligations and surrendering to the satisfaction of his artistic Chimera.

In pursuit of this dream, he managed to settle into an abandoned old barracks that a group of artists had occupied, located on the northern outskirts of Madrid, near the city's rail tracks. In one of the rooms, he set up a ramshackle studio where, along with his painting tools, he had a cot and the bare essentials to live. He participated in collective exhibitions held in the workshops of the barracks and occasionally in larger venues like Matadero or Tabacalera, loaned by the regional government to promote art among young people. He participated in international exchanges through networks fostering relationships between artists, particularly from various European countries, but also from America. He spent seasons in Paris and Berlin, exhibited in Italy and a number of northern European countries. It's hard to say if his artistic contribution was revolutionary, but what's undeniable is that Antonio was immersed in the search for a personal style. He experimented with different materials and themes, formats, and compositions, painting his canvases and repainting over them as if the value lay more in the search than in the finished piece. Along the way, he dabbled in psychoactive substances, which had gained in diversity compared to the monotonous absinthe of bohemia—alcohol now shared the spotlight with joints and other varied drugs, although in Antonio's case, rarely to excess.

He remembered those years with nostalgia. That period brought him to the highest peaks of creativity. He attended the Fine Arts school with a degree of regularity, and though Antonio's spirit was firmly anti-academic, that phase of study allowed him to devote a significant portion of his time to painting, which was then his top priority. He met countless people—some peers with whom he still kept in touch, others with whom he had quarreled over forgotten issues, resulting in the severing of ties. He was part of three or four groups of up-and-coming artists, one of which even garnered coverage in specialized magazines, all valid excuses for opening celebrations.

At some point—he couldn't pinpoint exactly when—mundane life began to take precedence over his artistic pursuits. He spent more time on self-promotion and socializing than advancing his painting. Several years passed where he walked a fine line of superficiality, but just as the ocean needs the deep sea to power the surface waves, Antonio needed to feel the pull of the abyssal Chimera to create his works. Gradually, he lost the appetite for painting. He created simple paintings to sell, and financial necessity pushed him into painting bourgeois portraits that pretended to be modern but were entirely devoid of originality. He found clients through a gallery owner with good connections who also gave him space in the gallery's catalog. The owner demanded more presence on social media and at public events—everything felt shallow and a bit hollow, covered in a superficial sheen meant to maintain his public image. He didn't earn much money, but enough to get by. Most of it was quickly spent maintaining his social calendar and renting a small studio in Carabanchel. Lulled by an easy life, he drifted along, and though it pained him at times to realize he had abandoned his artistic Chimera, he consoled himself with the thought that he hadn't betrayed any grand ideals—he had merely let life follow its natural course.

It was around this time that his partner became pregnant. Laura was a theater actress and a great fan of visual arts. Along with a mime and dance company, she had spent some time in the barracks where she and Antonio had staged performances with daring sets, combining choreography and avant-garde decor. Later, the theater world took her in other directions, and she toured countless festivals in various European cities. They had reunited about two years earlier at a farewell party before the barracks were demolished to make way for the city's northern expansion. Artists from all disciplines gathered to say goodbye to that building. When they saw each other, they smiled, as if their sole reason for attending was to meet again. They began talking, picking up the romance they had once started when they first met. Between drinks and dancing, they caught up on each other's careers—what they had been doing, where they had traveled, what plans they had for the future. It didn't take long for them to kiss, and by then, they knew their futures would be intertwined: After all these years apart, the time had come to move forward together.

With the night came the cold, and as they huddled together, they looked up at the sky, where a halo around the moon seemed to testify to the start of their relationship. They say that such halos form when moonlight refracts through ice crystals in the earth's atmosphere, and when the halo is particularly vivid, it's considered a sign of good luck. The truth is, they became one of those couples who were visibly comfortable with each other, clearly sharing a bond of love and respect—something sincere that survived in the depths of the chaos around them.

At first, their relationship wasn't so balanced, and Laura showed great patience with Antonio, as this period coincided with his years of partying and neglecting his art. That empty frivolity puzzled Laura, who had believed she had rediscovered the passionate young artist she had once known at the barracks. Instead, she realized he had become a disillusioned, mediocre artist, flirting with the illusion of fame and an elusive sense of recognition.

The news of the pregnancy brought Antonio to his senses. The child growing in Laura's belly embodied the essence and meaning of life that his work had been lacking. He began to abandon his wild lifestyle and drew closer to Laura, and as he moved away from his corrupted artistic Chimera, he grew closer to his partner, thrilled by the promise of love.

Financial pressures began to mount, and they needed a stable income and to settle down. Trying to make a living from dance and theater was a complicated prospect at that time, given their circumstances, and Antonio decided to turn to teaching in public schools. He secured a temporary position, which he accepted eagerly, and started teaching at the high school before their daughter was born. The job provided them with a regular paycheck, bringing the stability and security the family needed. They left Antonio's painting studio behind and rented a small apartment in La Latina. It wasn't large, but it was well laid out, and it had an extra room with beautiful light that streamed in through a large window above the neighborhood rooftops.

Once a week, Antonio would visit a nearby space used by local artists, where he would meet old acquaintances in an environment that brought back good memories. He tried to carve out a corner of the shared studio space, lent to him by a friend. He brought an easel and some of his supplies there, but in reality, he didn't paint much more than a few uninspired pieces. He was too involved in too many activities and associations that occupied his attention. He stayed busy responding to endless messages, social media notifications, and participating in countless projects. Antonio blamed his inability to return to painting on a lack of time—between his school job and the household chores he shared with his partner, he couldn't find the time to focus. However, the real problem was the distraction caused by being involved in so many things. It prevented him from deeply immersing himself in any of them, leading to a constant feeling of dissatisfaction, which pushed him to take on even more new tasks. This became a self-perpetuating cycle of busyness and superficial involvement, making him feel both incapable of dedicating himself to painting and plagued by a vague sense of emptiness.

For Laura, managing the household became her primary focus during the first year after giving birth, even though Antonio helped out with the baby and took care of some of the cooking and cleaning. As the year came to an end, Laura began seeking ways to resume her career. She became involved with a local dance academy where she taught a few classes and assisted with choreography. From there, she co-founded a small theater company with two fellow performers, neighbors from La Latina. They rehearsed in spaces they were allowed to use near the La Cebada market, and they planned to stage a production by the end of the year. Although she hadn't achieved her dream of becoming a renowned actress, she had found a more pragmatic balance: teaching at the academy and maintaining her passion for performance. In the past five years, they had staged two shows in independent venues with modest success, and they were now finalizing a third, which they hoped to perform soon. The company had built a respectable name in Madrid's theater scene.

This seemingly well-structured life was shattered by the news they received in late spring.

During a routine health check for safety reasons at Antonio's school, the results of his bloodwork showed an abnormality, and they asked him to repeat the tests. Antonio suggested waiting until after the second-semester exams, as the tests were scheduled for the following week and the classrooms had been set up with still-life arrangements for drawing exams. The doctors insisted he repeat the tests immediately, urging him to come to the hospital first thing in the morning. Once admitted, they didn't allow him to return home for clothes—40% of the cells in his blood were cancerous.

This abnormality also meant acute anemia, with hemoglobin levels far below what is considered critical. It meant that he could die from cardiac arrest at any moment. In fact, the doctors wondered how he was still alive. They immediately gave him two blood transfusions while Antonio called Laura to tell her to come to the hospital as soon as she could—there was startling news to share.

He spent the first month isolated in a room to receive radiation and chemotherapy treatments aimed at controlling the disease. The isolation was necessary because the treatments not only targeted the cancerous cells but also wiped out his healthy blood-producing cells in the bone marrow, leaving him with a severely weakened immune system. Medically, this is known as aplasia, a condition where the bone marrow stops producing blood cells. The physical discomfort is hard to describe: The toxic substances injected into his veins caused diarrhea, nausea, and vomiting, making Antonio feel like a stranger in his own body.

Though at first he thought he wouldn't be able to endure the pain, he soon learned that the capacity to bear suffering is something one can learn, and while it seems physical endurance is the key, the mind plays the leading role. The nights felt longer than the days, time dragged on between the nurses' checks (every three hours when things were going well, and almost continuously if complications arose). Some did appear, adding fever and discomfort to his already grueling ordeal, but the nurses explained that this was normal—the important thing was to find ways to cope with the pain in the current situation and to think positively about the future.

What helped Antonio most during these periods of suffering was thinking about Laura, their daughter, and his art. They kept in touch via video calls, and Laura was occasionally allowed to visit him in his clinical bubble. The little girl had grown, and they had explained to her that her father was sick but would soon get better. She needed to encourage him, make him laugh with funny stories, and have patience, knowing he would be home soon. Antonio had lost his hair and was very thin, but they told her that would pass quickly, and he would be back to normal in no time.

During one of her visits, Laura seemed anxious, rubbing her hands as if the synthetic hospital gown irritated her, and as she fidgeted, she nervously announced that she was pregnant. After celebrating the news, they did the math: it must have been the result of a particularly fun evening they had spent having dinner on an outdoor terrace at the beginning of the summer, just three weeks before Antonio had been admitted to the hospital. Their daughter had been staying with friends that weekend, and the two of them had reconnected in a slow, tender moment of intimacy.

The news gave Antonio a great deal of strength, especially as he was going through one of the hardest phases of chemotherapy. It was like a moral injection that helped him endure the treatment.

Thinking about painting helped him tremendously, as he tried to figure out how to represent pain and the relief that followed it, the delirium he experienced during febrile episodes, and the dreamlike images that appeared after doses of morphine. When he was clear-headed, he made notes in a small notebook, capturing these sporadic experiences before they faded from his memory. He sketched in a drawing pad, composing forms and imagining colors with a box of pastels Laura had brought him.

He had completely abandoned social media, and the work-related messages had stopped being important since they coincided with the end of the school year and his medical leave. In those circumstances, he could dedicate his time to thinking about whatever he wanted, free to imagine without restrictions. Paradoxically, despite being confined to a hospital room, he felt as though his horizon had expanded, and disconnecting from the trivial routines of daily life allowed him to reclaim his time, and with it, the space for his mind to roam freely.

Every morning, after the nurses completed their 6:30 AM check, he would close his eyes and meditate. First, he concentrated on his breathing, feeling the inhalation and exhalation of air through his mouth and nose. Then, he would relax all his muscles, imagining a veil slowly rising from his feet, gradually uncovering his entire body. Afterward, he mentally scanned his weary limbs, feeling the blood pulsing through his veins. Thump, thump, thump. When the pulse reached his head, he observed his thoughts as they passed before him, and by choosing a pleasant memory, he allowed himself to be transported as if he were free, outside the hospital. In this way, he flew over Mediterranean beaches, relived hikes through lush mountains, and re-experienced endless colorful sunsets that gave him the strength to face another day within the hospital walls.

For Laura, reorganizing her life was not easy. She had to take on all the household chores she could no longer share with Antonio, particularly caring for their daughter, who had been used to spending much of her time with her father. When the school year ended in summer, Laura enrolled her in a day camp, though Laura still had to pick her up in the afternoon and keep her entertained until bedtime.

Laura remained involved with the academy and her theater group, and staying focused on preparing for their show's premiere became her top priority. As long as the pregnancy allowed, she didn't want to miss any rehearsals. However, she now had to add hospital visits to her routine, along with managing Antonio's fluctuating mood and the constantly changing news about his health. Some days brought hopeful signs of improvement, only to be followed by frustrating setbacks.

After a month in the hospital, Antonio was sent home, a situation that quickly became untenable and turned into frustration. Physically, he was still very weak and completely dependent on others. On top of that, the unpredictable fevers could spike at any moment, forcing them to rush back to the emergency room.

Faced with these circumstances, they opted to have him readmitted for a second round of chemotherapy. Although this one was lighter, it was necessary to control the disease. Overall, the doctors were pleased with his progress and believed he was responding well—the first onslaught of leukemia had been stopped in time. The initial treatments achieved the expected results: The cancer cells in his blood had significantly decreased, and the spread to other vital organs was under control.

At this point, a genetic analysis of the blasts had been completed, revealing the mutations responsible for his disease. This allowed the doctors to make a more personalized diagnosis. The leukemia was classified as acute and aggressive. It would return in the coming months, and controlling it with radiation or chemotherapy wouldn't be easy. They could monitor it and try to keep it at manageable levels for several months, but turning it into a chronic illness seemed impossible. Most likely, the leukemia would come back, stronger and more aggressive than before.

The proposed solution was a bone marrow transplant, or more accurately, a stem cell transplant to restore his blood production. Given the characteristics of his leukemia, the process of finding a donor and obtaining approval for the transplant was expedited. A full report on his condition was submitted, along with tests to certify that the rest of his organs were healthy. After an initial period of uncertainty, a donor was found in the United Kingdom, and the transplant was approved by the regional medical committee. Antonio was aware of the risks of these procedures and was filled with fear and doubt. He knew the process would be long and painful, with the possibility of transplant rejection or, in some cases, death. Ultimately, however, he followed the advice of his medical team and decided that a new bone marrow was worth trading Spanish tapas for the British tradition of afternoon tea.

The transplant proved to be even more grueling than the previous treatments: five weeks in isolation in a small room after undergoing chemotherapy to destroy his original bone marrow. The intense suffering required high doses of morphine to help him cope with the physical pain.

During this time, Antonio arrived at the hospital well-prepared. He brought with him his notebook, his drawing pad, his pastels, and his ink supplies, hoping they would allow him to better capture some of the images going through his mind. He used the rare moments when he felt well to paint and stoically endured the difficult times, knowing they would pass.

There was one particularly challenging phase when Antonio developed septicemia—a severe bacterial infection in the blood—that left him in poor condition, making the doctors fear for his life. During this time, he stopped painting and was never able to pick it up again. His hand trembled and he found it difficult to hold the pencil. Now that his spirits were low, he lost the comfort that painting brought him; misfortunes always come accompanied. The septicemia left him bedridden and delirious, but he knew he had to endure; he thought of the good things that awaited him at the end of this battle, and he eliminated pessimistic thoughts just like the restorer tirelessly removes layers of old varnish from a painting.

When possible, Laura visited him, wrapped in those acrylic hospital garments to prevent her from introducing germs from the outside. She settled into a chair away from the bed, maintaining a safety distance. These forced conditions of separation and distance were a harsh test that united them even more. It is curious how sex is a corollary of physical attraction, but it is words that strengthens love. They talked mostly about their memories and their daughter, never about the future, because it seemed dishonest to make plans under those circumstances.

They remembered that cold night in the sapper barracks when, embraced under the halo of the moon, they committed to a common future. They relived their daughter's stages of development, how she had gone from stumbling while skating down the hallway to performing pirouettes on her skateboard in the park circuit. When Laura left the room, she felt sad, leaving him alone in his suffering, not knowing how to help him; however, Antonio, with each of those visits, recharged his batteries to face the unpredictable shocks that awaited him.

Each morning, he returned to his meditation, delighting in his most pleasant memories, observing how his mind organized his positive thoughts. He evoked his memories, upon which he built his present.

Antonio gradually regained strength. The doctors were optimistic and encouraged him to believe he was approaching the end of the tunnel; the exit from that first phase of healing was near. The next step would be a slow recovery at home, accompanied by a methodical follow-up with outpatient visits.

He was tremendously weak, and when he showered, he looked at his body and thought of the illustrations of orphanages from the postwar period. His muscle mass was almost imperceptible; he suffered dizziness and cramps if he tried to stand up to exercise. Aware that maintaining his physical condition at a minimal level was important, he used the little strength he had left to make movements in bed to avoid injuries in the lumbar and cervical regions. He had no energy left to paint or organize his supplies, not even to hold the brushes with his trembling hand; nevertheless, he continued to play with the images in his head during the periods of drowsiness, and in the brief moments when he felt clear-headed, he took notes in his notebook, which rested on the bedside table.

He was discharged from the hospital on a bright day in early autumn. A gentle breeze caressed his face as he crossed the glass doors leading to the street, and a faint smile appeared on his face, hidden under the protective mask he was required to wear. In light of that first satisfaction that flooded him, he soon had to temper his optimism upon seeing how small limitations turned into large hurdles difficult to bypass. Walking to the taxi was an odyssey, and getting up to his apartment was a struggle, despite having the support of an orderly who accompanied him. Sitting on the sofa at home, he felt calm, but as soon as he tried to get up to go to the kitchen, he felt that his legs could not support his weight, he lost his balance and sought support to prevent the inevitable fall.

He tried to appear normal in front of his daughter so as not to scare her, but the girl noticed her father's fragile state and was ready to care for him as diligently as one of the hospital nurses; she brought him a glass of water, handed him his cane or a book. Antonio was overwhelmed by a feeling of uselessness that increased as he saw Laura, already five months pregnant, having to shoulder all the household chores in addition to the burden of caring for him. He felt like a burden, and there were several occasions when he wished he had remained hospitalized, where at least he was not a load for anyone. Recovery was going to be slow and long; improvements would come gradually, so a few months lay ahead during which everyone would have to muster a lot of patience.

It was not just Antonio's impression; Laura was indeed overwhelmed by her situation and also by what lay ahead. After giving birth to their first daughter, she had struggled to organize her schedule to balance motherhood with her budding professional activity, and now that it seemed she was managing to put together an interesting project, it was going to be difficult to carry it out. She was not someone who liked to give up before trying, but making a realistic assessment, she saw it as impossible to hold the premiere before giving birth. It was not so much about being pregnant; if no problems arose, she planned to stay active until the last day, just as she had during her first pregnancy. She was very aware of the limitations entailed during the first months and relied on the help her colleagues would provide. It was more about the feeling of being alone, of having fallen into the trap that women of her mother's generation fell into: sacrificing her personal life for that of the family as a whole. She had always viewed the couple as a shared life project and believed she had chosen a man with whom to realize it. But it seemed that this damn illness was determined to take away her plans, and there was little she could do without being seen as a selfish person.

Antonio was on sick leave from work, and except for two days a week when he visited the hospital for clinical check-ups, he had all day for his recovery. The priority was physical exercises to gain independence of movement, a matter of perseverance that he achieved thanks to his motivation. Every day, lying on a mat, he did crunches and back exercises; then he used weights and bands to develop a minimum amount of muscle in his arms and chest; afterward, squats and push-ups to strengthen his legs. He went out to the starway of his building and first went down, then went back up. One, two, three, up to eight steps down, leaning against the wall to avoid falling. One, two, three, up to eight steps up, holding onto the railing.

After a month, he was able to go buy bread on his own, slowly advancing down the street, proudly holding the loaf. In the following weeks, he reached new goals that were a challenge for him, although they were ordinary for anybody else, such as doing the full grocery shopping and walking his daughter to school.

Eating was difficult at first, and cooking was impossible; the smells made him nauseous, and he vomited by merely getting close to food. Little by little, he began to increase his tolerance, first to the simplest foods, then to a wider range. His goal was to replace Laura as the cook. It took time, but after two months, he was able to take full charge of the household chores, planning the weekly menus, buying what was necessary, and cooking. All these daily achievements increased his confidence in recovering his life and making Laura's more bearable. He did so slowly and calmly, with long naps at noon during which he slept soundly.

During the recovery period, he also dedicated himself to poring over books that had been on his reading list. He made frequent visits to the library to borrow old titles he had pending, as if they had been waiting for him on the shelves for this moment. Curiously, he reduced his relationship with social networks to a minimum, just enough to send messages to those closest to him about his health progress. Contrary to what he would have done before the illness, he did not log on continuously to read news or update himself on multiple topics that only captivated him fleetingly.

Just as he had felt pleasure in regaining his physical form and performing domestic chores, he experienced it when regaining control of his time, rejoicing in thinking about nothing or rereading a book while enjoying a good coffee. And in that monotonous calm, it seemed that his mind was gaining the ability to stop and delve into the essence of things. His capacity for observation was expanding; he appreciated the different colors and shapes. He let his mind be inactive, in a state of contemplation, and delighted in the calm of waiting. Slowly, images arrived that organized themselves, and Antonio, a mere observer, reveled in their contemplation.

One midday in the Madrid winter, Antonio approached the window of the additional room in his house and let that sea of light, colors, and shapes enter his retina and flood his brain with optical sensations. The rows of Roman tiles formed intersecting planes depending on the distance and orientation of the rooftops, like folds in a dress fitted to the figure it conceals. In the background, off to one side, a "corrala" rose two stories above the other buildings, revealing its communal hallways. The doors of the apartments separated by wooden beams, created a theatrical backdrop where two people wandered, and another smoked leaning on the railing. In front of him, clothes dried in the sun, hanging from three balconies, adding a note of color and movement that contrasted with the stillness of the view. Dominating the scene was a dome, standing out against the deep blue sky, its slate tiles slipping down the sides beneath the lantern. Black, violet, or gray depending on the angle.

Antonio was experiencing a new sensitivity, one that seemed to have been heightened after his illness. It was as if the hazy layer of chasing fame, the need to impress others, and the pressure to be present in social circles had been erased. And as the fog lifted, a blank canvas appeared, receptive to the tiny details reflected in the light, the subtle traces of movement left in the air, the unique combination of colors and shapes that formed every moment. He picked up a piece of charcoal in his fragile right hand and, with determination, sketched the composition of his next painting on the canvas. He didn't hesitate for a moment; he accepted what he was creating with full confidence, working without hurry on the canvas.

That afternoon, he prepared his tools, checked his brushes, cleaned his paint rollers, inspected his oil paints, and examined some new ones he had been gifted. The next morning, he returned to the sketched painting, applying the brushes and colors with a primal satisfaction. It was as if he knew exactly what tone he needed at every moment. He searched the palette patiently, with delight, and confirmed with pleasure that he had managed to express what he wanted to convey. Like Monet circling the pond and water lilies in his retreat at Giverny, Antonio circled the light and movement of his urban terrace. He had finally achieved what he had sought for so long: using painting to express the union of feelings and thoughts that often escape representation, but when captured tangibly, leave the undeniable certainty of success.

The following days, he painted whenever he had time between his dedication to household chores and taking care of his daughter, morning and afternoon. The studio, abandoned for so long, filled with drawings and paintings. He experimented with forms and materials he had never dared use before, exploring a balance of colors that allowed him new forms of expression. He was able to express everything that had accumulated inside him during his illness. The memory of pain and uncertainty reminded him of life's fragility and the pleasure of enjoying every moment. His paintings evoked the resilience of his struggle to move forward, and they soon evolved to reflect the complexity of human emotions, not only in the face of illness but in the difficult situations many people encounter in their daily lives.

One evening, Laura returned from her theater rehearsal, which had completely absorbed her over the past few months. The play she was directing was set to premiere in a few weeks, and after much effort, it would debut before the baby was born. She wanted to be there for the opening and the first performances before going on maternity leave and letting the company carry on without her. Being able to let go of much of the household burden had greatly helped her make progress with the production, and barring any unforeseen issues, they should stay on schedule. She needed a few more weeks to polish some details and give it one last push, after which she would figure out how to organize everything. She opened the door, hung up her coat, and slowly walked toward the living room, letting her thoughts shift to domestic matters.

Antonio approached her, coming out of the studio. He was wearing an old, paint-stained shirt and a pair of torn pants she hadn't seen him wear in ages. Laura was delighted—she had been worried that Antonio wouldn't be able to regain his passion for art, and those clothes were an unmistakable sign that he had been busy with his painting tools.

He offered her some tea, and they sat together in the kitchen; their daughter was at a birthday party, and they had some time to talk.

"I've started painting," Antonio revealed hesitantly. "This time, I'm painting in a different way. I do it with an ease that reminds me of when I was a teenager, letting myself be swept away by sudden inspiration. I capture what I want to express on the canvas with simplicity and confidence" - his voice grew more animated as he spoke. "It's as if the journey through physical pain and mental suffering has slowly distilled a way to express myself with a style that's truly my own. As if the physical helplessness and weakness, the disconnection from the outside world, had pushed me to focus inward."

She listened warmly, with affection, sensing that he needed to be heard. She'd noticed for a while how he'd been withdrawing into his own world, his small tasks. Their daughter was grateful for it; she was engaged in her activities and happy with her friends. The food at home was much better—fantastic lentils, vegetables cooked to perfection, as if prepared by a true chef. But it was time to leave the cave, to express what he had experienced.

"I am determined to start painting again," Antonio said, clenching his fists with resolve. "I'll request a leave of absence from work, but I'll also take care of the kids so you can continue with your job. I'll change the baby's diapers and wipe his nose [5]; I'll take our daughter to school and do her homework with her. All I ask is that once I'm done with the household tasks, you let me paint alone in my studio. That you allow me, in those moments, to enter the creative madness and, isolated, let myself be touched by the breath of the chimera."

Laura stood up and went into the studio, where she looked at the scattered sketches pinned to the wall and two paintings propped in a corner that immediately caught her attention for the beauty of their composition. She circled the dirty easel positioned in the corner and cracked open the shutter to better observe in the evening light a large painting that Antonio had just finished. As she admired it, she lifted her head and saw the brightness in Antonio's eyes. She realized the painting was brilliant, and his hesitant gaze was asking for her support to continue.

She slowly moved toward him and, with a gentle yet firm gesture, took him into her welcoming arms. In contrast to the chimera's embrace, this one was grounded in reality, with its limitations and dreams, with its law of gravity. They remained in the embrace as night fell, and when they finally pulled their heads apart, near the window, they saw the bright halo of the moon glowing once again.

III

Human chimeras

"Medical or human chimera" refers to a person whose body is composed of organs from two different entities. Therefore, this includes all living beings who have undergone transplantation of a vital organ—such as bone marrow—or have received transplanted limbs. According to the latest data I consulted[7], based on reports from national transplant organizations, more than 6,000 organ transplants are performed annually in Spain, and worldwide, the number is approaching 160,000. The most common are kidney transplants, but liver, lung, and heart transplants are also included. To this, we must add allogeneic bone marrow transplants, where the patient receives transplanted stem cells from a donor. These number around 1,300 per year in Spain[7] and approximately 40,000 worldwide[9].

Overall, the number of transplants has increased by about 8% in recent years. It is difficult to know whether this increase is a post-pandemic effect linked to the decrease in transplants during COVID-19 or whether it reflects a steady trend. In any case, my goal is not to provide a rigorous review of numbers, as they can vary depending on the source. Rather, I want to highlight that soon, the number of new human chimeras in the world will be close to 200,000 per year[7]. While this is a small percentage of the population, it is still a significant number. We can confidently say that the 21st century is the century of chimeras.

As I mentioned, what unites human chimeras is having gone through a delicate health situation, where we have felt both the fear of losing our lives and the deep pain involved in the healing process. I hope that both of these feelings will diminish for future transplant recipients. Medical advances are reducing the risks of these procedures, and perhaps the suffering will become more bearable, though for now, it remains an inevitable ordeal.

There are other perceptions that are common to chimerism. On one hand, you become aware that your life continues thanks to the generosity of others, specifically the donor. The donor might be a close family member, as is the case with some kidney or bone marrow transplants, but in most cases, the donations are anonymous and altruistic. Some donations are made while the donor is still alive; a healthy person signs a living will, in which they donate their organs for the benefit of others. Other donations are consented to by relatives at the deathbed following an accident. In Spain, up to 86% of families authorize the use of a loved one's organs for transplant after a fatal accident[7]. The idea that these organs, which will soon stop functioning in the person who has passed away, can save or improve the life of a stranger is an act of generosity that speaks of the goodness of human nature and reconciles us with our often-questioned species. It seems that, when we set our minds to it, we are a *Homo sapiens* species that knows how to prioritize the well-being of humanity.

On the other hand, you are the result of the knowledge that has been accumulated over many years by medicine. The first transplants began experimentally in the mid-20th century, and it wasn't until the end of the century that long-term survival rates improved significantly. This opened the door for these therapies to be extended to many countries and a broad segment of the population. Advances in knowledge have come slowly and continue to do so, requiring the efforts of thousands of researchers worldwide and the necessary funding.

The creation of national and international associations for organ collection and stem cell banks has played a fundamental role in exchanging resources and combating incompatibility. Equally important is the work of healthcare teams who have direct contact with patients and deserve special recognition. How can we not feel indebted to those who have made transplants a viable reality? Every human chimera is aware of what they owe and feels a sense of obligation to give something back to society, even if they don't always know how to do so.

As is true for all chimeras, human chimeras are marked by fragility—the risk that their new state might break down and become non-functional. In the early stages, there is the issue of graft-versus-host disease, commonly known as rejection, in which the donor's organ rejects the recipient's body. Occasionally, it may be the recipient's cells that recognize the donor's cells as foreign and activate the immune system to destroy them.

For decades, this was one of the main reasons transplants were not viable, but today, this issue can be mitigated through drugs that control the immune system. It requires individualized monitoring of each patient, and

in many cases, the reactions are limited to dermato-
logical issues, digestive system disturbances, or fever
during the first hundred days after the transplant. Of
course, more serious complications can arise, and close
monitoring is necessary. Complete failure is not out of
the question, whether due to a recurrence of the original disease or the death of the patient.

In bone marrow transplants, the immune system re-
covers very slowly, which can lead to all kinds of short-
and long-term infections. In organ transplants, total
rejection is also a possibility. Complete recovery is considered to occur five years after the procedure, though
there is always the real or imagined dread that it could
happen again.

Doctors often tell us that a transplant tends to come
with a process of aging. The body goes through difficult
situations that tend to leave a mark, and the mind wan-
ders down reflective paths it is not accustomed to. This
aging is more pronounced in adults than in young people, but for both, it translates into a unique experience
that will affect how we face life going forward.

What is this new way of facing life? I don't think
there is a single answer. Each individual must find their
own way, based on generosity, fragility, and vulnera-
bility. However, I dare to say that chimeras can play a
significant role in today's society, which is characterized
by a rushed sense of time, information overload, and
overwhelming technology that tends to diminish the individual. The role of chimeras could be to renew a vital
humanism by recovering the essential values of being
human. We can use the time that recovery grants us to
reflect on how to repay our debt to society and to ensure
that, in this rebirth, we avoid repeating past mistakes.

The future offers the possibility of more sophisticated and stranger chimeras emerging, capable of saving many lives. I am referring to the transplantation of organs from animals to humans. Specifically, pigs have the greatest potential as donors due to their significant biological similarities to our species. For some beliefs and religions, this kind of interspecies organ exchange causes revulsion, as do organ or limb transplants between different human bodies. Once again, we are confronted with that repulsion toward chimeras for what is strange and mysterious. The rejection of what we struggle to comprehend persists.

Perhaps at the core of this chimeric challenge lies the acceptance of different people within society—not just medical chimeras, but also those who think and see the world differently. We might ask ourselves: What is collective progress if not the acceptance of differences, the creation of a diverse society that accommodates the various individuals who compose it? This is the vital humanism to which new medical chimeras can contribute—the kind that seeks to include gender, racial, or belief diversity, because what truly matters is the essence of the human being.

As we already know, the combination of different realities introduces weakness, and there is always the risk that a chimera will break down and cease to be functional. That's why chimeric societies haven't survived, why they are impossible dreams, and why human chimeras were considered unrealizable for so many centuries.

How to make chimeras viable in the long term remains a challenge without a clear answer. It requires active participation to minimize rejections, and although modern medicine has managed to resolve many cases, there are still many in which success has not been achieved.

Complications

Before entering the operating room, I already knew that the survival rates after a lung transplant were lower compared to other grafts. My doctors explained this to me as I deserved, as a fellow professional, with general statistics—ones that, broadly speaking, I already knew—and tailored to my specific case, which was particularly complicated. I was prepared for a slow and difficult recovery; it might not even be complete.

Some people think that doctors don't get sick, and that if we do, we suffer less. Nothing could be further from the truth. Under normal conditions, we get sick just like everyone else, and if there are epidemic conditions, we are more likely to get infected due to greater exposure. But what's curious is that when we do get sick, we are more reluctant to admit it. We struggle to juggle the dual role of doctor and patient. With mild symptoms, it's common for us to rely on self-diagnosis and self-medication. We refuse to acknowledge that we're ill and we keep going to work, driven by professional duty. If the discomfort seems to worsen, we'll consult a colleague in the hallway over coffee or during a break. In short, we're far from being an example of how to properly manage illness.

One thing we do have going for us is that we analyze the illness rationally and have the knowledge to understand the processes we are going through and predict how they might evolve. However, we shouldn't overestimate this ability, because in many cases, ignorance is a good companion—especially if the patient is in good hands and willing to follow the advice of a medical team.

In my case, I leaned heavily on the second option and let myself be treated calmly. It's true that there were times when I had arguments with my colleagues—not so much to defend a different point of view, but to better understand what was happening to me. The progression of the disease was rapid; I lost abilities within days, leaving me confused and disoriented.

From the moment I realized the illness was threatening my life and I began to suffer intense physical pain, I felt a strong desire to write, which is where these pages come from. I can't explain why; it could have been the need to record a unique experience that was subjecting me to extreme tests. It could have been the desire to leave something behind for my loved ones and for others who might go through a similar situation. Or, it could simply have been a desire to leave for myself a clear trace to escape the hateful oblivion of my fragile memory. Even today, I don't know why. It may be because I feel the risk of dying or being deeply limited for the rest of my days, and I rebel against it through these notes. Or, more simply and directly, it could be that I'm taking advantage of the therapeutic power of writing. Please understand that I'm referring to literature as the selfish act of writing, drafting for oneself, letting the feelings and thoughts expressed on the blank pages help heal the patient, just as colors and shapes brushed onto a canvas heal the artist. So, if you read these notes, don't expect academic perfection. Don't look for sophisticated rhetoric or refined style—just let yourself be carried by the irregular pulse of a voice anxious to express itself.

I'm rather short—exactly 1.58 meters—and I've always been on the thin side. In fact, I've maintained a very proportionate figure throughout my life. My face could be described as that of a smart girl, with very lively brown eyes that, according to my boyfriends, seem to sparkle. I have a large, clear forehead, thin eyebrows that lead to an elegant nose and mouth, framed by a well-defined, perhaps overly prominent jawline. In other words, I'm attractive, though not with striking features, and even now, past fifty, I've managed to keep a youthful, lively, and intelligent expression. Of course, I have some flaws, both physical and in my character, but I won't mention those in these pages because it's not a matter of digging myself into a hole.

I've wanted to be a doctor since I was very young. In my family, there was only one doctor—my grandfather's brother, whom I admired. He was a very large man with a beard, kind, and he spoke to us children as if we were adults, but always with a good sense of humor. He rarely participated in heated family discussions, but when he did, he spoke calmly, and everyone went quiet to listen to him. His input always soothed the conversation, often steering it from passionate tangents toward reasonable discussions.

One summer, at the pool, a group of boys rescued a child two years younger than me, who was drowning and had lost consciousness. Back then, there were no lifeguards at pools, so my great-uncle had to push through the crowd of panicked people to get closer. He laid the boy on his back and began moving his arms. When that didn't work, he placed his gnarled hands on the base of the sternum and pressed down repeatedly on the chest until the boy finally expelled water from his mouth and began to breathe. I was fascinated by the calm and determination with which he acted. He knew exactly what to do at each moment, amidst the screams, cries, and chaos. If I could choose my role in a similar situation, I wanted to be the calm that contrasts with the chaos. That's why, when people asked me why I wanted to study medicine, I would answer, "Because I like healing people."

I remember my university years as a period of intense study and almost monastic seclusion, during which I immersed myself in books, acquiring knowledge that we occasionally applied in practical seminars. There's something strange about that initial phase of education, where a uniform group of students is trained to think and analyze using common cognitive foundations, following the same patterns. It's as if the ideal of a professional group striving to advance in service to society were a flock of starlings moving in synchronized formation. In human reality, however, many dissonant elements appear—individuals with their peculiarities that would prevent the flock of birds from forming its extravagant shapes but allow the profession to progress as a whole. I adapted well to that combination of uniformity within the medical body we were becoming and the individuality of its members. I didn't mind sacrificing a significant part of my dedication if it meant I still had time to excel in the areas where I wanted to stand out personally.

Then came the specialization. Thanks to my good grades, I was able to choose my favorite field—hematology—and I trained at an excellent hospital in Madrid. I spent four years in the oncology and hematology ward, seeing patients with a wide variety of conditions, all dealing with difficult-to-understand and hard-to-accept diseases. Some patients had very determined personalities and approached their illness like a fight, a battle between two roosters—the patient and the cancer—facing off in the same body.

Others, who had already experienced a relapse after initially promising results, dealt with their situation with more resignation. They adapted to their limitations without losing hope. I remember Ramón, who suffered from recurrent sarcomas in his bones, which had limited the mobility in his legs. After six months of outpatient treatment, he was admitted to the hospital for a final attempt at a cure, but just before the procedure, a hospital-acquired lung infection forced the treatment to be stopped. They had to go back to square one and come up with an alternative strategy to tackle the disease. How hard that was to accept, and with what strength he endured it! He had been a concierge at a two-star hotel and spent his afternoons learning English on a mobile app, a long-standing goal that might help him travel in some improbable future.

Then there were the optimistic newcomers, who seemed to view the disease as if from outside their bodies, as though they couldn't quite believe that this recently learned diagnosis would define their future. The most moving cases were the young people who discovered in their thirties that cancer had affected seven of their organs. It's hard to grasp. Your life collapses like a house of cards—fragile, unstable. As a doctor, you try to hold the cards up with flailing gestures, knowing it's useless and only a matter of time before it all crumbles.

Finally, there were the veteran patients, those who knew their future was limited, accepting palliative treatments as a last resort for devastating prognoses. I remember a man about sixty-five years old who refused to endure the hardships of a second liver transplant and asked to be sent home. After explaining the situation to his daughter over the phone, he hung up and told his partner, "She only cares about the inheritance, as if she'll get more than her siblings." I was leaving the room after treating the patient in the neighboring bed, and hearing him say that filled me with deep sadness. It's hard to witness how such dark emotions can dominate a person's final moments.

It was in that ward that I completed my training as both a doctor and a person, learning about the complexity of human reactions when faced with extreme situations.

What I didn't expect was that one day, I would find myself lying in a bed with a terminal diagnosis, just like any other patient. The illness that brought me to this point was pulmonary hypertension, which I had been suffering from for years. I can't say exactly when it started, because if I search my memory, I'd been showing symptoms for a long time. Fatigue, dizziness, even chest pressure, which I attributed to tiredness or respiratory allergies. One day, while at the hospital with some colleagues, I felt a slight dizziness and woke up in the intensive care unit. They told me I had fainted while we were talking, and I had been unconscious for three weeks. The test results were unequivocal—I had advanced pulmonary arterial hypertension. The causes weren't clear, and for the time being, they were going to try to improve my symptoms so I could feel better. A few days later, they moved me to a shared room in the pulmonology unit and prescribed medication for me.

In the initial phase, I responded well to the treatment, to the point where they discharged me from the hospital on the condition that I remain on medical leave from work and attend regular outpatient check-ups.

I returned home like a soldier coming back from battle. My mother, who had already passed away, wasn't there to welcome me, but my daughter was, and she greeted me with a warm hug. The familiar spaces and furniture that I usually didn't pay much attention to took on a comforting presence, as if they had been waiting for me. Sitting in my favorite chair by the window, I rested my legs on a leather footstool shaped like a bulldog and spent my time watching the branches sway in the autumn sunlight. My daughter would ask me what I was thinking about. She could see my happy smile, my peaceful stillness, and wasn't sure whether to worry about my unusual inactivity or be glad that I was following the medical advice for my recovery. I reassured her: I could spend hours without thinking about anything, simply enjoying the homely feeling the objects around me gave me, and the calmness of familiar spaces.

As I gradually improved, I began creating a new routine. I did some light exercises in the morning to maintain my muscle tone and breathing exercises in the afternoon to encourage lung activity. I started taking daily walks and, through perseverance, first managed to walk around the block without assistance, then to climb uphill streets on my own, and eventually to carry light loads of items up the stairs. Regaining my physical form made me feel like I had control over my body and the illness—it gave me the strength to continue reclaiming my desire to enjoy life.

I also gradually regained my mental activity. I'm lucky to have a stimulating job that constantly offers learning opportunities. Having time to catch up on advancements in my field of specialization was a luxury I missed amidst the daily hospital hustle. I reviewed pending literature, organized databases I had been compiling from my work, which had piled up in my computer files. To the astonishment of my colleagues, I even wrote a scientific article, distributed it for their review, and submitted it to a journal for publication.

In the afternoons, I set aside time for literature. I've always loved reading, both novels and essays, and now I had the opportunity to indulge in it. I started with some new books I had been meaning to read, but soon I fell into the joy of re-reading. I would search through my not-too-large but well-stocked library of favorites and immerse myself in the books like reconnecting with an old, dear friend. I rediscovered the pleasure of reading slowly, savoring a precise description, the introduction of a character, or the unfolding of a narrative plot. I delighted in putting myself in the author's shoes, trying to guess their next steps in the writing. I became aware that some of the books I considered my favorites had been read hastily, without appreciating the richness and intelligence they held. Now, I had the chance to dive into them with calm and extract what I had overlooked in my previous readings. Recovering from an illness gives you the opportunity to revisit familiar places with a different perspective—the illusion of revisiting places thinking you won't make the same mistakes as yesterday, the chimera of being reborn wiser and, therefore, free from repeating past errors.

After a few months, I was able to drive and took my daughter to a small cabin we have in the mountains, surrounded by trees and lost in the middle of nowhere. When we bought it, it was an old stone and wood house in terrible condition, but it was in a beautiful location, isolated in a meadow surrounded by forests with magnificent views that made us forget the city. It's a place I've always loved. My partner and I began visiting it shortly after finishing our university studies, and we rebuilt it almost entirely with our own hands. For the roof, we had to hire a team of local workers who built the structure with seasoned pine beams and laid the traditional tiles of the area, flipped upside down, as is done in Segovia where it snows.

We loved being close to nature, and we were clear that it was something we wanted to pass on to our daughter. Taking a hike in the woods until we were exhausted, picking wild mushrooms to share later at dinner with friends, enjoying the warmth of the fireplace on a cold afternoon—these small pleasures have accompanied me throughout my life, and just thinking about them brings back wonderful memories. We've managed to pass some of that on, as my daughter told me that when she feels nervous about an exam or is stressed, she calms down by thinking about the smell of blackberry jam that would fill our kitchen in September, when we made preserves from the freshly picked berries.

Returning to this cabin after being in the hospital was like re-reading my books. I would sit, entranced, looking at a wooden beam, imagining animal shapes in the knots or doodles in the grain. I would sit on the terrace, looking at a familiar view as if I were seeing it for the first time. Revisiting even the smallest details gave them a new meaning that filled me with satisfaction. I then decided to test whether visiting more spectacular places that had always impressed me before the illness would have an even greater impact.

We went on a hike, though it couldn't be to the mountain peaks, as my lungs would tire, so we went to a waterfall that cascaded down a granite gorge, creating a torrent. As we got closer, I could feel the humidity in the air increasing, the vegetation becoming lusher, and the smell of wet earth. When we reached the edge of a crystal-clear pool, into which a vibrant horsetail of water fell, crowned with a rainbow in two different arcs, I was mesmerized. It's hard to say whether it was the accumulation of sensations I experienced in that moment or the memories that rushed through my mind from previous visits, but I felt intoxicated. That hike alone justified our trip to the mountain house. On the drive back, I found myself thinking that having gone through the illness was, in some ways, positive, as it gave me the great advantage of heightening my experiences and appreciating pleasures that had become dulled through repetition.

If I'm recounting activities that bring me joy, I can't overlook one of my great passions: flying light aircraft. I've been fascinated by it since I was young. I think it began with my admiration for the first female aviators—intrepid, adventurous women who represented independence better than anyone else. I don't mean to discredit the merits of the suffragists, but for me, nothing compares to a solitary aviator from the early 20th century when it comes to models of determined and liberated women. So, as soon as I turned 18, I threw myself to the "West with the night"[5] starting with ultralight classes at an airfield near my hometown, then passing the exams for my first flight and radio operator licenses. Today, I still maintain my private pilot's license, and whenever I have time or need a boost to lift me out of the monotony of life, I go to fly a small plane.

The view from the air of familiar places is always changing. On a foggy day, a faint mist reveals glimpses of the landscape; on a sunny day, the green stands out after the rain. Nature is constantly transforming, and from a bird's-eye view, you can appreciate all the changes it presents, despite its apparent stillness. It's a privilege to enjoy this spectacle of metamorphosis, which is visible to all but only fully savored by those flying and the birds around us.

The moment of landing the plane is particularly exhilarating. It begins when you spot the runway and plan the landing operation. Over time, it becomes a combination of instinct and reason, requiring your full attention. As you check in with the radio about traffic on the airfield's runways, you visually identify other aircraft in the circuit, the presence of birds nearby, the intensity and direction of wind gusts. In a matter of seconds, you make decisions about what to do: flight speed, angle of approach, wind correction. As you glide over the runway, just before losing the plane's lift, you feel a flutter in your stomach, driven by the stress that demands the full engagement of your mind and senses. So, every time I descend from the cockpit and set foot on the ground, I feel as though I'm still floating for a while, and when I return to my regular life, I continue to feel like I'm gliding through the air while performing the most routine tasks.

Given all this, it's easy to understand that one of the experiences I wanted to have after the illness was to fly. It wasn't something I could explain to my daughter, who has always considered it a reckless hobby even under normal circumstances, so there was no point in discussing it during my recovery. I know my fellow doctors well: While they're prepared for various situations, it's better not to ask about things that might receive a negative response. The most reasonable route I considered was a harmless lie that, without hurting anyone, could bring me great satisfaction. I told my daughter that I was going to my office at the hospital that morning to download some data from the computer, which could be useful for an article. I'd be home just before lunchtime. I had already arranged to meet a pilot instructor friend at the airfield early in the morning so he could accompany me on the flight; I may be daring, but I'm not reckless, despite what my daughter might think. By mid-morning, on a splendid, sunny winter day in Madrid, we were taking off, heading toward the mountains.

Those cold days with blue skies are wonderful for flying. The dense air helps the plane float, and the limitless visibility fuels the pilot's imagination. You can even spot animals wandering among the oak trees in the pastures below. Once again, I felt immense pleasure, just like in front of the waterfall. The sensations piled up, giving me a sense of complete freedom—happiness must be something very similar. I made a flawless landing, with subtle movements of the controls. Like a skilled surgeon, I adapted to the wind and the runway, touching down as gently as a bird. Wonderful. At home, I confessed my little adventure to my daughter. It cost me a good scolding, but I took it like a mischievous child who is fully aware of the price she will have to pay for her mischief. What would life be without these great pleasures?

To complete the review of the experiences that brought me joy during my recovery, I must mention music. I'm sure it's much more accessible to most people than flying light aircraft, and it was a permanent and irreplaceable companion throughout my healing process. I've always been a great music lover, although primarily as a listener. I've tried to play various instruments, but with little success, as I'm not gifted for performance. I hear the melody in my head and can even hum it, but while it sounds great to me, those listening are unable to recognize it. I'm not talking about a sophisticated aria or symphony; even when I hum "Once Upon a Time, There Was a Little Boat," no one can guess what I'm singing. It's frustrating, but I compensate with the immense pleasure I get from listening to music.

I enjoy varied styles depending on the circumstances. In classical music, I'm partial to Baroque, and my favorites are cello and string concerts or combinations with the harpsichord. That's not to say I don't love Mozart and Mahler, or that I'm not passionate about Italian opera arias and avant-garde composers from the early 20th century. In modern music, jazz and flamenco are my favorites, and the fusion of the two ranks among my top choices. I can listen for hours to a 1950s American saxophone or a timeless Andalusian guitar. And if it's about listening to rock, pop, Latin, African, or reggae rhythms—bring it on, I'm up for anything. Let's say I'm somewhere between eclectic and a music lover overall. Each music for its moment, and each moment, its music.

As with my other pleasures, illness has enhanced my ability to enjoy a good album. Many afternoons, I would sit on the couch in the living room, facing the window, listening to music. The week before my last hospital admission, I had planned to test that sensitivity by attending a chamber concert in a nearby Renaissance church with fantastic acoustics. Unfortunately, that wasn't possible because my condition worsened considerably. The dizziness and chronic fatigue returned, preventing me from leading a normal life.

This relapse was particularly difficult to overcome. The doctors tried various medications to control the disease, but they couldn't stop its progression. I struggled to breathe, suffered from increasingly frequent shortness of breath, and felt my heart race to compensate for the lack of oxygen. The causes of my pulmonary hypertension were unknown. I wasn't overweight, nor did I have other factors that would make me prone to it. There were some ancestors in my family with respiratory problems, but since detailed diagnoses weren't made in their time, I can't say for sure whether there was a genetic component.

Finally, as my condition worsened and given my relative youth, I was put on the waiting list for a lung transplant. Once approved, I had to wait for available organs, and about three months ago, I received lungs from a donor who had died in a car accident.

The surgery went well, according to what my colleagues explained to me, and despite all the discomfort it caused, the initial prognosis was favorable. But knowing the potential complications that can arise from a transplant like this, many thoughts about life's fragility passed through my mind. As a doctor, I'm used to dealing with death and always keep it in mind as a possible outcome in some of the cases I handle. As a person, I can't help but feel fear, even though I knew the transplant was the best option for me. It was an irrational fear that struck me at unexpected moments, during the day or night; I would endure it helplessly as it hit me, waiting for it to pass, like a strong wave that surprises you when you're walking into the sea. It's not worth resisting—you let yourself be tossed around until the waters calm, and your mind is ready to reflect.

The first thing that came to my mind was concern for my loved ones, especially my daughter, who would be left alone. But she's already grown up; she's finished university and started her internships. I have no doubt she'll be a great professional—she's organized and very calm. Financially, she will inherit living in our apartment and enjoy the cabin in the mountains. I have spoken with a notary and arranged both the donation of my properties and my will. If things go wrong, it will be very simple for her. I'm sure she'll find someone who loves and appreciates her. I hope she has children with him. When I look back, that's what has brought me the most satisfaction. Perhaps what hurt me the most at that moment was thinking that I wouldn't meet my grandchildren or enjoy a few more years of life.

The second thing that came to mind were the things I hadn't done—trips I had always postponed, which never happened, friends I had lost touch with due to carelessness, and most importantly, reconciliation with my sister. Disagreements in the last years of my mother's life had led to an absurd estrangement between us, so deep that we didn't know how to break it. We had a very good relationship during our childhood and youth, with the usual sibling squabbles, of course, but always strong support for each other on important matters.

Once we each left home, we started living our lives in our own ways, and for reasons I can't piece together, we drifted apart. I'm sure much of the blame was mine. I become so obsessed with my work that I neglect those around me. It's not that I'm uninterested in what others do, much less out of disdain; it's just that, since I feel completely confident in what I'm doing and don't need anyone's approval or admiration, I assume everyone around me feels the same way.

I had to correct this when raising my daughter because I realized she needed to hear words of encouragement from her mother—words of affection, of attention. Those words didn't come naturally to me, and when faced with those teary eyes begging for a response, I had to invent them. I thought of my great-uncle, the doctor, and the confidence he conveyed when he spoke to me as a child, the calm his words brought to family conversations. Maybe my words sounded a bit artificial at first, but since they were well-received, I gradually incorporated them into my usual way of speaking.

This time, I'm trying a similar strategy with both my sister and my daughter. I push myself to express my affection for them, and as I do, I feel a growing desire to open up and express more of my feelings. In short, once the emotional storm had passed, my response to death was the will to correct my past mistakes, fulfill some unrealized dreams, and make amends with my loved ones. These were reasons enough to keep fighting for life while maintaining a healthy respect for death.

Like all transplant patients, after the graft, I had to undergo immunotherapy to prevent potential rejections that could result in the loss of the organ. The body that receives the transplant identifies the presence of foreign elements with a different genetic composition and activates its immune system to destroy those cells as a defense mechanism. To prevent this natural reaction, the patient's immune system is suppressed with medication. However, a body without defenses is more exposed to infections and the development of cancer cells that, under normal conditions, would be controlled by the immune system. In other words, immunosuppression must be carefully balanced—it must be strong enough to prevent the deterioration of the grafted organ but not so strong that the body can't defend itself against infections or cancer. This balance is key to ensuring the transplant's long-term survival. For decades, acute rejection or infections were the leading cause of mortality in transplant patients. Chimeras offer the possibility of healing but also carry with them inherent instability.

In lung transplants, the issue of infections is particularly serious, as the organ is in constant contact with the outside environment. Bacteria, fungi, or viruses can enter through the air we breathe. That's why, to minimize risks and avoid overuse of immunosuppressants, it's common to isolate patients after the transplant in disinfected rooms with restricted access to healthcare personnel and systems that inject purified air. These are like bubbles where contact with the outside world is minimized for as long as necessary until the patient develops enough strength to protect themselves. I was very familiar with these systems since, in my hematology specialty, clinical isolation is frequently used after bone marrow transplants, which also result in a loss of the patient's defenses. However, when it was my turn to experience isolation, I realized how mentally and physically challenging it can be.

I have been confined to a small room of about twenty square meters for three months. There was an attempt to transfer me home, but it only lasted two short days before it became quickly unfeasible. Most of the time, I spend lying in bed, even though light exercise is necessary for my recovery and to prevent fluid buildup in my lungs. That's why, whenever I get a break from the suffering, I try to do a set of physical exercises I've created based on my physiotherapy sessions and the Pilates classes I used to do when I was healthy. I start by gently working my lower back and neck while lying in bed, then I get up and walk around the room, taking with me the stand holding my medication and IV fluids. It's a huge effort, but it strengthens the hope that I still have control over my body, that as long as I have the will to move and take care of myself, I will be able to pull through.

There are bad days when the pain prevents me from doing exercises. I try to be kind to myself, but if several days of inactivity stack up, my morale drops, and I have to make a double effort to get back into my exercise routine. When I can, I sit in the armchair next to the window, which, though closed and six floors up, allows me to watch the mysterious movement of people and the repetitive traffic below. Often, I accompany it with music, which either soothes or quickens my thoughts, depending on my mood. Distraction keeps me occupied during the day. In my better moments, I read some of the books I've brought on an electronic device, and when I get tired, I watch movies or read the news on the computer.

The night is long. The nurses come in periodically to change my medications and IV fluids or to check my vital signs. Sleep comes only in brief snatches, or I drift in and out of a semi-conscious state, filling the time with memories to make it pass faster. Daydreaming helps, and in these moments, I imagine myself standing in front of the mountain waterfall, feeling the mist on my face, on a newly conquered peak above a sea of clouds, or piloting a small plane over an endless runway. Anything goes to trick yourself into this game where the most important thing is that time passes and recovery draws nearer.

In my case, despite all the precautions, the bubble couldn't prevent a latent infection from a virus already inside my body from being triggered. It was hidden within cells acting as a reservoir, and as they began to proliferate, they developed a pneumonia. At first, I didn't experience any discomfort or particular symptoms, but after a while, I had difficulties breathing, and then a deep unease set in.

The medical team has been doing everything possible to stop it, but the disease continues to progress. Recently, they informed me of a grim terminal prognosis: The pneumonia is winning the battle, and there's little left to do. The next step will be palliative care to help me cope with the situation—waiting for death, which is now inevitable.

I've asked to be taken out of the clinical bubble and moved to a regular room. In the best-case scenario, the isolation would only extend the waiting by a few days—it's not worth it. In these final moments, I'd rather be near my daughter, for her to hold my hand when my strength fades and I start to lose consciousness, for her to share her warmth with me as I near the cold.

My physical limitations are increasing, so I'm forced to finish writing these notes that have supported me so much during this journey. I can barely hold the pen between my fingers, and the notebook slips from my hands. It's too late now to switch to typing them, so I'll ask my daughter to transcribe these notes into the computer while she waits by the bed. I find comfort in thinking that perhaps reading them can help patients who walk a similar path.

Before concluding, I'd like to make it clear that fighting for survival is essential in all illnesses, especially when the prognosis isn't favorable. Attitude isn't everything, but when it's positive, it can help you pull through. The success rate of transplants is very high nowadays, and while it's undeniable that there are associated risks, most patients recover well. So, although I haven't had that luck, it's important to keep spirits high and trust that a transplant recipient can become a long-term viable chimera.

To increase that likelihood, I've made sure to sign the consent for organ donation. It seems that most of my organs are in good condition, and therefore can be used to save or improve the quality of life for others.

I forgot to say, this is Marta. Remember me among the fighters who face death with calm acceptance.

Here ends my story.

IV

Creation of chimeras

As we continue to uncover previously hidden aspects, I hope the reader begins to find chimeras more appealing or attractive. Beings that initially repel us gradually reveal their charms as we get to know their less superficial layers. By peeling back their outer coats, we uncover the reasoning behind their configuration—the origin of their inherent duality, which gives them a determined yet fragile dimension. Once we overcome this apparent fragility, chimeras can help solve previously unsolvable problems. Expanding the term, chimeras could also be architectural, geopolitical, linguistic, and countless other variants across various fields of knowledge.

In a burst of optimism, we might create chimeras to solve problems that couldn't be resolved in other ways. This requires an active attitude and a willingness to create. Let's consider, for example, the role they could play in incorporating monuments from despised historical periods or from actions that are less than honorable into the collective memory of a society. Creating a chimera from these monuments would allow us to preserve them, but with a new critical interpretation that enriches their historical and contemporary significance. Aesthetically, the result might be questionable, but in terms of memory, it could still be valid if it opens the door to a more optimistic future.

An example of chimeras of this kind could be the early Christian buildings that began to appear in the second century, during the persecution of Christianity. Like the Chimera, they emerged underground in Rome, in the catacombs, where sepulchers or mausoleums were transformed into places of worship for the new, forbidden religion. In the fourth century, when Roman emperors made Christianity the official religion, these early Christian buildings multiplied and spread throughout the empire. They emerged on the surface and were created by adapting ancient Roman, and even Greek, temples or buildings. This led to fascinating structures that served as a bridge between classical architecture and the new styles that appeared in the medieval period. These buildings gave rise to Carolingian, Visigoth, and Lombard architecture, which formed the foundation of later Western architecture. They were also the predecessors of Byzantine architecture, which followed an independent evolution. Hence, our admiration for chimeras like the Cathedral of Syracuse or the more modest baptisteries and pantheons transformed into places of worship across the Mediterranean. Consciously or unconsciously, these early Christian chimeras laid the foundation for much of modern architecture.

On a more current scale, perhaps the chimera that remains the greatest geopolitical challenge of the 21st century is the solution to the Israeli-Palestinian conflict. Unresolved since the creation of the State of Israel, the Oslo Accords proposed in 1993 the chimera of two states as a pragmatic solution to allow both peoples to coexist. As a chimera that inherently carries its own weaknesses, it has not been implemented—at least not as of this year, 2024, a year marked by terrible warfare in those territories. After the accords, one of their signatories, Yitzhak Rabin, was assassinated by an extremist compatriot. All attempts to put it into practice have been weak and unsuccessful or simply aborted.

Experts in this conflict say that the Taba Summit in 2001 brought representatives from both peoples closer to an agreement than ever before, but subsequent events made it unfeasible. However, the path remains open, and it is probably still the only viable solution to the problem.

Currently, only a portion of Israel's population supports the two-state solution, while the extremist government in power rejects it. It is necessary for Western countries, particularly the European Union and the United States, to strongly support the progressive minorities in Israel who back the idea. Furthermore, those of us who support and appreciate Israel must clearly convey that this is the only valid solution: Supporting the coexistence of two states is supporting Zionism and Jewish society.

If we have succeeded in modern medicine in keeping human chimeras alive, why couldn't we manage to solve a geopolitical chimera? We know that chimeras carry within them the potential for weakness and self-destruction, which is why they require greater effort to become viable. States would need to be redesigned so that both territories could be independent, past mistakes avoided, and a great deal of goodwill put forth by the participating peoples. But it is possible, and it could open a door to hope.

Another great chimera is the European Union, created to avoid repeating the dramatic conflicts of the 20th century, which continues into the 21st century with its firm yet fragile duality. Its vigorous identity is undeniable—not only as a major market and economic power but also as a beacon of human rights and values that serves as a reference to the rest of the world. We won't delve here into its past atrocities of colonialism, slavery, and certain old ideologies that are ethically indefensible today. The reality, despite all that, is that out of those experiences has emerged one of the most open, free, and creative societies in human history.

The union of states willing to cede part of their sovereignty in favor of a higher geopolitical entity lies at the foundation of its creation, while the rejection that occurs between them forms the basis of its fragility—a chimera with multiple heads that requires continuous effort to maintain its viability. The European Union has made no shortage of mistakes and missteps, which its critics have seized upon to call for its dissolution and demand a return to greater national sovereignty.

Nonetheless, the collective civic and social achievements are undeniable. Those of us who were condemned to live much of the 20th century under dictatorial regimes—whether right-wing or left-wing—have felt it especially in the democratic opening of our societies. Europeans as a whole can attest to this, having enjoyed the longest period of peace in their recent history. The challenge of viability remains, especially now as we witness, with disbelief, a new war in Ucrania—one that experts warn could spread and escalate beyond what we could imagine. This war was unthinkable for many of us just a few years ago, and the possibility of it escalating is unimaginable. The European Union acts hesitantly in the face of these threats, but we hope that, in the medium term, it will strengthen its solid and compact nature, rooted in the principles of its founding.

Here are examples of how chimeras based on reason can be possible. No longer would they be monsters born of dark, irrational, and mysterious forces but rather the result of rational imagination offering solutions to seemingly unsolvable contemporary problems. The supposed contradiction in the dual meaning of the word chimera begins to make sense under the logic of the 21st century.

The chimera of hope

My name is Yuval Peres. When my family moved to the kibbutz of Ramat David, I was ten years old, and I still clearly remember the impression it made on me. Located in northern Israel, it resembled a town planned by an urbanist, with its neatly arranged houses, each with its own garden area. The houses were well-kept, painted in pastel colors, with a single story, and divided into two homes. You entered through a three-step staircase that led to a central porch with two side doors, each the entrance to one of the homes. We were assigned the one on the right, which had two bedrooms, in addition to the kitchen, bathroom, and living room. It would be more accurate to say that the kibbutz assigned the house to us—it wasn't ours. By being accepted as members of the kibbutz, we were given accommodation. At that time, all property, including homes, service areas, and production means, belonged to the community. Our individual belongings were limited to a few personal items we had brought from Argentina and some small household goods we bought with the surplus from the monthly allowance the kibbutz provided to each family unit.

The gardens were green, with well-maintained plants and flowers—something I hadn't expected, as I thought we were moving to a very dry country with water shortages. There were large trees providing shade, making it pleasant to walk along the paths connecting the houses. The main streets that crisscrossed the space were paved, illuminated at night, and lined with greenery. For us, coming from a chaotic Argentine city, this level of order and harmony was new—we weren't used to such well-organized spaces.

When I became older, I learned that Ramat David was founded in 1926 by Central Europeans. The walls featured photographs of their arrival to this semi-desert region. Set up in tents, the first settlers began working the land and establishing an agricultural commune based on socialist Zionist principles. They tapped into three natural springs connected to the aquifer of the Jezreel Valley and started working an old, abandoned orchard with basic tools. The photos showed young men and women dressed in light cotton clothing, performing various farming tasks. Most of these youths had no experience, as they came from Jewish urban communities involved in commerce and liberal professions. They managed to transform the land they settled on, first building barracks, and later, more sophisticated houses and buildings that were still in use.

Little by little, they diversified their activities. By the time we arrived, the main sources of income were pear and cotton farming, along with a dairy farm that allowed us to sell milk to a nearby kibbutz, which paid us with a variety of dairy products. In terms of technology, we had specialized in manufacturing trailers for various agricultural uses, which we sold to other kibbutzim, and, though to a lesser extent, self-propelled irrigation machines powered by hydraulic energy and programmed with the support of small solar panels. Considering that the population had progressively grown and stabilized around the current seven hundred inhabitants, it was hard not to admire those early immigrants who, through their efforts, settled in this barren land.

At the center of the kibbutz was the main building, which housed the communal kitchens and dining areas. Every day we went there to have breakfast, lunch, and dinner, where we met with other kibbutz members, sitting at long, shared tables. When we went to school, we also ate in the communal dining hall, though they organized separate shifts to avoid coinciding with the adults.

Sometimes we cooked simple dishes at home, like cakes or pastries for birthday celebrations or similar events. We invited neighbors or friends and hosted a small anniversary party among our closest ones. For these occasions, we bought food at the commissary, a store located in a building near the dining areas where we could purchase some groceries and everyday items. But most celebrations were held communally, either with the rest of the kibbutz residents or with a subgroup we formed, often based on age.

Work was divided among all members according to the kibbutz's needs and each person's abilities. Every Friday, the organization's secretary posted a list on a board at the dining hall entrance, assigning tasks to each person for the following week. You could be assigned to gardening, cooking, fieldwork, or other duties. Most of us rotated between different positions, although some had specific functions assigned when it was considered appropriate, or when there were particular conditions that required it. During pear harvest season, a lot of manpower was needed in the orchard—even the kibbutz's general secretary had to go out and harvest when it was his turn. I liked this rotation system because it allowed us to get to know the people we worked with, including those in leadership positions, and it also kept us from always doing the same job.

The factory and the dairy required specialized personnel. Those who weren't specialized performed support tasks, allowing them to understand how these centers operated and to be aware of their importance to our community. I began to be assigned tasks at the factory when I was seventeen years old. There was an occasion when a machine broke down and needed to be unclogged. I had some knowledge of mechanics and have always been good at it, so I helped fix it and get it running. Besides, I showed that I was capable of operating the machines and could handle the physical work well, I was given more and more responsibilities. So, on the weekly list, the name Yuval Peres began appearing more and more frequently assigned to the workshop.

Working at the factory was interesting because the metallurgy section hired Arabs from nearby villages to reinforce the workforce. They arrived at the kibbutz early in the morning and left at the end of the day, bringing their own food, which they ate in a room designated as a canteen. They spoke Arabic among themselves and Hebrew with us, but during the breaks we merged all together and chatted in their language to create a close and friendly relationship.

I was told that Ramat David had to pay a fee to the national kibbutz association for each external salaried worker—a kind of penalty for relying on external labor to use our means of production. It was a topic of debate because some kibbutz members disagreed with hiring outside workers and believed that all production should be based on internal labor. Others, however, argued that besides allowing us to maintain trailer production—one of our main sources of income—it also fulfilled a social role by creating jobs for our Palestinian neighbors. A meeting was held specifically to discuss the issue, attended by all adult kibbutz members, where the economic results were presented, outlining the advantages and penalties of hiring external workers. After three hours of discussion, with arguments for and against, a vote was held, and the majority decided in favor of hiring external workers. Decisions were always made democratically, from electing the general secretary to any matter that significantly affected the community's operations.

Another group of workers we received were foreigners who came to stay with us. Most were Jews from the U.S. and France who spent the summer working in the kibbutz in the mornings and studying Hebrew in the afternoons. There were also agriculture students or the like from other countries who came to spend time learning about our organization and operations. I'm not sure if "workers" is the right word, "visitors" might fit better. While it's true that we included them in our community and they appeared on the task assignment lists like all the members, it was clear they weren't used to physical labor. Though most of them made an effort to adapt, their contribution was limited. In the summer, we would wake up at dawn to start working by five. We took a break at eight for breakfast, and then we worked until noon. It wasn't a schedule these visitors were used to.

However, we enjoyed hosting them because they were young people with whom we spent our free time in the afternoons at the pool, playing soccer, or engaging in other leisure activities. They told us about life in their home countries and gave us an external perspective that was fascinating. What interested us most was the Americans' point of view since almost every young person in the kibbutz dreamed of leaving after military service and moving to the U.S. Personally, I didn't feel that urge to leave the country—perhaps because I had lived in Argentina during my childhood and was very comfortable here. However, many of my peers were born in the kibbutz, and the only trips they had taken were school outings, so their need to leave was pressing.

In any case, don't get the wrong idea about what I'm saying—we were far from being a claustrophobic group, isolated within ourselves. On the contrary, we were young people who dreamed of seeing the world. We had access to television channels, concerts, and movies brought to the kibbutz, and even exhibitions by artists who were occasionally invited. Moreover, the education we received at school was very open and prepared us for whichever future we wanted to pursue.

Collective education was deeply tied to the kibbutz's development. The individual was respected, but always educated within a group. When the kibbutz was founded, the collective spirit was even stronger. Babies were separated from their parents a few months after birth and raised by specialized women in a designated area. By the time I arrived in the 1980s, that practice had already disappeared, and children stayed with their parents until the age of twelve. They attended school, spending most of the day with other children, but afterward, they returned home to their families.

Another characteristic of the education that later

became very relevant in my life is that it was fundamentally secular. It was heavily focused on the acquisition of basic knowledge in sciences and humanities, preparing us to perform the tasks needed in the kibbutz, while also opening the door for us to choose other options in the future. Judaism was taught from a cultural perspective, where we learned and analyzed traditions while minimizing the religious aspects. We studied the history of the Jewish people, their various diasporas, and branches, but all from a secular point of view. Within the kibbutz, we felt very distant from the Orthodox Jews who had such a significant presence in Jerusalem. In fact, many adults displayed animosity toward them, considering them "lazy" because they didn't work their whole lives and lived off the contributions of others. For us, dignity was acquired through work, and our role in society was determined by our contribution to its production.

At the age of twelve, we moved to an area where we lived with our peers until we were sixteen. I remember it as the best period of my life! We ruled that territory by ourselves. We lived in small houses—in pairs—that opened onto a garden where we had a common area to meet. In that area, we had arranged stones as seats in the shape of a Greek amphitheater, and we used it to discuss topics or perform various acts, from comedies to musical performances. When any of us living there wanted to say something, we would go to the center of the scene, attract attention, and have an audience ready to listen.

Next to the makeshift theater, there was a large tree that provided shade in the summer, which had become the symbol of our independence, standing tall in the center of the garden. We young people who lived there shared our concerns and decisions, and we also organized everything without anyone's help. We used the space as we saw fit, whether choosing where we wanted to sleep or setting rules for the common area. We also managed our own time, adapting it to the kibbutz's obligations like school or dining, but then allowing each person to use their free time however they wished. We organized group activities as well. No adult from the outside could make decisions about the matters of our little world, except when a major problem arose and some members turned to an external person to mediate the situation. In those circumstances, we learned how to live together, experienced our first loves and arguments, and built dreams of escape and the future—it's hard to imagine better conditions for a person's development.

Between the ages of sixteen and seventeen, we moved to the regular kibbutz housing, living in groups of four roommates. Responsibilities increased as we were added to the work schedule and had to perform tasks while continuing our professional education. We started thinking about what we wanted to do for a living and what our future plans were.

Joining the military at eighteen was something most young people eagerly anticipated, though I must admit I didn't share that enthusiasm. I fulfilled my three years of military service out of obligation, not with passion. I was never drawn to weapons or violence, and while I understood the important role they played in society, I was always more interested in exploring peaceful solutions. In our kibbutz, there were night patrols as a preventive measure, and after completing the initial part of military service, we were placed on the patrol rotation, performing armed rounds in pairs every night. It was a security task, during which I never had to fire a shot or challenge anyone.

There were people in the kibbutz who had fought in wars, and some who had even been decorated. For example, one of the boys, slightly older than me, had participated in the First Lebanon War. He was wounded during one of the skirmishes and was treated like a hero. We all admired him and treated him with great respect, being patient when he had fits of anger, and trying to calm him when nightmares haunted him at night. His stories were our direct testimony of real war, and they had more to do with hardship, sacrifice, and suffering than with the heroism they tried to instill in us through television and military service. In any case, the training period I completed in the army was interesting and taught me a lot about life; I met many boys and girls from other backgrounds with whom I exchanged opinions on a wide variety of topics, apart from our military activities. Plus, we had leave time when we would return to the kibbutz, where the younger ones looked at us with admiration as we recounted our exploits, and the adults with respect for our fulfilled duty.

A few months after finishing military service, I began working at a computer company. I took some intensive courses to complement my previous training and was integrated into the workforce. Unfortunately, when I was about to complete a year of work, routine medical tests unexpectedly detected anomalies in my blood. They told me I had severe anemia, which could lead to a lack of oxygen in vital organs, including the heart, and could result in lethal heart failure. After being urgently admitted to the hospital, they quickly ran tests and concluded that I had acute myeloid leukemia. Half of the cells in my blood were blasts, a type of cancerous cell that, besides being non-functional, attacked healthy cells. The disease was aggressive, and it had to be urgently controlled before it could cause problems in other organs.

I was transferred to the Sheba Cancer Center, near Tel Aviv, where I was assigned a team of experts in treating these diseases. First, they subjected me to induction chemotherapy, and once they managed to reduce the number of blasts below an acceptable limit, they put me through a second round of consolidation chemotherapy. After this process—which lasted almost three months—they warned me that the chances of the disease recurring were high. The problem lay in my bone marrow: It produced highly malignant cancer cells that learned from the treatments, so with each recurrence, it would be more difficult to control them through chemotherapy. The solution was a bone marrow transplant.

All options were considered. The first was an autologous transplant, where healthy cells produced by my own marrow were harvested and, once confirmed to be healthy, used to replace the diseased cells. The process was long and painful, as they destroyed my diseased bone cells through a combination of radiation and chemotherapy. It didn't work. I can't explain the medical reasons, but the reality is that after all the suffering, the treatment didn't work. At the same time, a compatibility study was conducted with my close relatives, but no match was found.

The next step was the bone marrow registry, an organization that collects samples from anonymous donors to form a large national database, increasing the chances of finding a compatible individual. The information-matching process is carried out using computational genetics techniques, and in my specific case, a one hundred percent compatible donor was found, opening the door to a definitive cure. Although the information is completely anonymous and confidential, in this case, the registry was forced to give me some details: the donor was a young Palestinian, and therefore my express approval was required to receive the marrow transplant.

"Yuval, it's the only sample we've found that can guarantee a high level of success for the transplant," the doctor told me. Then he continued, head lowered, as if embarrassed by his second suggestion, "We could consult with banks in Europe, but it would take a long time and delay the procedure. Our recommendation is that you accept the marrow we're offering you."

I didn't hesitate for a second. The efforts of my parents and the kibbutz to give me a secular education did me a great favor. I gave my consent without hesitation.

A few months before the turn of the millennium, I had to endure the ordeal of having my bone marrow suppressed again to make way for the donor's. It's a pain you never get used to, but you endure it because you know it's the solution and that if you want to stay alive, you must endure the agony. The important thing is that the new stem cells took root properly and began producing healthy blood that circulated throughout my body. I've never quite understood how the old marrow is replaced by the new one, and even less how my diseased blood is replaced by healthy blood. I've tried to imagine it, but it remains a mystery. My blood type changed—I had been A positive all my life, and after a few months, I became O negative. I visualize the blood in my arms, legs, stomach, liver, and other organs being replaced by the new blood, like subway passengers replacing those who leave the train cars.

What's hardest for me to imagine is how this process occurs in the brain, which is irrigated by countless tiny capillaries. I suppose all of them empty out and refill with the new plasma. Where does the old blood go? Am I still the same person as before? Do I think and reason the same way? Medically, these changes are explainable, although I must admit that even though it's been explained to me several times, I still don't fully understand it. Psychologically, they are transformations that have a deep impact, and when combined with a period of suffering in which you are highly sensitive, they leave a profound, indefinable, but tangible mark.

For people with a strong religious belief, perhaps these processes are easier to accept—they can turn to a benevolent god who clarifies or justifies what has happened. Those who have replaced religion with more modern spirituality also find something to hold onto—this abstract spiritual idea provides great help in making sense of the senseless. The solution seems to be simple and so I told myself:

"Yuval, become a religious person, or at least develop beliefs about the afterlife that will help you cope with this situation."

However, those of us with a materialistic tendency are forced to explain the process solely through the rational nature of the human being. This humanism gives us the strength of reason, but at the same time, it limits our capacity for comfort. All we know is that we owe our new life to those who have helped us, but we don't know how to thank them. What I would give to know!

Once the transplant's success was confirmed, I was discharged from the hospital and only had to return for outpatient visits, where I underwent periodic tests. They monitored for cancer cells and conducted chimerism tests, which involved measuring the proportion of my blood and bone marrow cells that originated from the donor. After eight months, all my blood cells were from the donor. My hemoglobin, platelet, and white blood cell levels were already high, and after a year, they returned to healthy ranges. The monitoring would continue for the next five years, but the remission of the disease was considered complete.

The final steps of my recovery coincided with the second Intifada. While I was having blood drawn for a monitoring test in September, I saw on the television in the blood bank room how, following Ariel Sharon's visit to the Temple Mount, Palestinians threw stones at Jews praying at the Western Wall. Israeli police quickly responded with live ammunition. Afterward, violent riots and street battles broke out, lasting until the end of the year. That fall, I was called up to serve as a reservist in the Israeli army. First, I was sent to East Jerusalem, where I patrolled the streets and was involved in several urban clashes. Later, I was deployed to the West Bank, where I witnessed the deaths of both fellow Israeli soldiers and the Palestinians we were fighting against.

As the conflict progressed, it became increasingly difficult for me to understand the reasons for that war. Perhaps that's not the right way to express it: I understood that we were fighting for the survival of our people and that it was necessary to ensure the safety of our citizens. The Jewish people have suffered enormous cruelties throughout history, and we have the right to

defend ourselves and fight for a land that was ours before it belonged to the Arabs. I had learned this premise
in school as a child, and I had lived it firsthand during
my childhood and youth in the kibbutz.

When I was a child, some of the founding settlers
of Ramat David were still alive, and they told stories of
their flight from Europe and their settlement on the land
that they later worked and made their own. It was land
they had purchased with donations and that belonged
to them as members of the kibbutz association. While
that right to our country seemed indisputable to me,
doubts began to arise about the way we implemented
it, and I increasingly felt disconnected from how we defended it. There came a point when my doubts became
so strong that I could no longer push them aside—they
would strike at the most unexpected moments, hindering my ability to respond.

The first time my military duties were interfered
with was when I couldn't pull the trigger during a violent Palestinian demonstration. Many of the protestors
were very young, but no less dangerous because of that.
I knew I had to fire to keep them at bay and prevent
greater harm, but I found it impossible, and it was the
other soldiers in my battalion who took care of it.

The second time was during a surveillance patrol
with four of my fellow soldiers. We were ambushed just
outside Ramallah, and I froze when I locked eyes with a
boy throwing a rock at me. The last thing I remember is
a sharp blow to my temple, and then I collapsed unconscious. When I came to, dusk was falling, and we had
regrouped at a camp far from the city. I was lying on a
stretcher in the infirmary, my head pounding, and when
I reached up to my forehead, I felt a bandage. Pulling my

hand back, I saw my fingers damp and stained with blood. They told me it wasn't serious, that I needed to care for and disinfect the wound to avoid complications, but I could leave when I felt better.

After a few minutes, I decided to get up and take a walk around the camp to clear my head before returning to my tent. I reached the place where a metal fence with concertina wire had been set up to hold prisoners. Inside was the boy who had thrown the stone at me. He got scared when he recognized me and stepped back, thinking I had come to get revenge. I offered him a cigarette; he came closer, took it through the fence, and I lit it for him in a gesture of camaraderie. I tried to speak to him using the Arabic I had learned from the workers at the trailer factory.

"I'm Yuval. What's your name?" I spoke slowly and enunciated carefully, accompanying my words with gestures.

"-Mohamed. I am Mohamed," he replied and then took a deep drag on the cigarette.

"Are you from Ramallah? Have you always lived in the West Bank?"

"Always. My family used to live near the coast, in what is now Haifa. They had to move in the fifties," Mohamed said. "I was born near Ramallah twenty years ago."

"Have you ever gone back?"

"When I was little, we went to the sea. We used to go to Acre Beach. There's a photograph of the cousins at the beach; I'm six years old, and we're all smiling," he took another drag on his cigarette, a nostalgic smile appearing on his face.

"They took us to that beach on school outings. I loved it. I remember the little black tar beads, solid as pearls in the cold water, sticking to your feet when you walked on the dry sand. As you left the beach, there were brushes where you'd scrub the soles of your feet to remove them."

"On your feet and on your towel. My mother would scold us when we'd return the towel with those black stains stuck to it. She'd make us scrub them off before we put them away."

"For us, she'd put us on the stairs out of the house with a basin of solvent and wouldn't let us in until we'd scrubbed off all the tar balls. Even the ones on the soles of our beach shoes."

"Those were the worst. The heat would make them fuse to the rubber sole, and there was no way to get them off," we laughed together, connected by the memory.

"Once, they buried me in the sand, leaving only my head out and making a star shape around me," Mohamed said, staring off into the distance. "When I dug myself out, I had black marks on my shoulders and back. I got a real scolding for it! My mother scrubbed me down until my skin was raw." We laughed again, picturing his skin all smudged.

We both took a drag of our cigarettes. A comfortable silence fell between us. I seized the moment to shift the conversation, hoping for a genuine response.

"Why do you throw stones at us?" I asked. "You know you can't win. The best you can hope for is to be taken prisoner, like what happened to you," I added in a gentle tone, trying to sound sympathetic.

"For dignity. We resist for dignity," he said, looking at me with his penetrating, dark eyes, proud yet defeated. "We'll do everything we can to keep you from getting your way. This is our land. Do you know I can no longer go back to Acre Beach?"

His voice rose with excitement, drawing the attention of the guard, who called me over. He was a fellow soldier I'd known for years. He walked over briskly and spoke to me in a reproachful tone.

"Yuval! How can you be talking with the Palestinian after what you did?" he asked, with evident annoyance in his voice. Then he ran his hand over the charger of his rifle hanging across his chest. "You endangered the whole patrol with your inaction."

I was frozen, not knowing what to say, while Mohamed slipped away quietly, blending in with the other prisoners.

"I risked my own life after you got hit in the head with that rock to save you from being captured," he said, grabbing me by the collar of my uniform and dragging me away from the Palestinians on the ground. Meanwhile, the other soldiers gave me disapproving looks. "Have you lost your mind? What's with trying to strike up a conversation with the prisoner?"

I stayed silent, tried to respond, but no words came out. I closed my eyes and looked down at my feet, my expression a mix of shame and regret. I didn't even know what was happening to me.

"That's not even considering the possibility you were planning something worse, like freeing him or something like that," he shouted, voice filled with anger. My attitude wasn't helping; it was making him nervous, pushing him toward aggression. "Get out of here!"

I walked toward the tent without looking at the soldiers who murmured disapprovingly as I passed. A feeling of guilt that kept me from sleeping stayed with me all night. When we returned to the barracks, I decided to seek psychological help within the army.

My service record was spotless. I had fulfilled all my duties in the military, and I was promoted to sergeant for my competence in difficult situations and for earning the respect of my comrades. At first, the psychologists attributed my mental blocks to exhaustion; however, they decided to delve deeper into the reasons with some psychoanalysis sessions. When I explained my theories about the effect of chimerism on my behavior, they were surprised.

"Palestinian blood runs through my veins, which, besides saving my life at a crucial moment, continuously nourishes my brain," I told them casually, something they already knew. "Every time I see the dark, deep gaze of a young Palestinian fixed on me, I can't help but think that perhaps he is the donor of my bone marrow. From that moment on, I freeze, forget my military training, and my duties seem to dissolve."

"Look, Yuval, all of that is just your assumptions. The fact that you have a Palestinian donor should not affect your behavior at all," they replied kindly but firmly. "You're confusing scientifically proven biomedical facts with psychological reactions. Your behavior is completely independent of the origin of your marrow."

"I understand, and I know what you're trying to convey to me," I ran my hand over my shaved head before continuing. "I share the reasoning, but when it comes to action, a deep, primal feeling awakens inside me that paralyzes me."

"You have to overcome it. The first step is to correct your thinking. If, as you say, you understand that these assumptions of yours don't make sense, you need to act accordingly. Try it. If we see that it doesn't work, we'll find another way to approach it."

They cleared me for duty, and I returned to my battalion. I first carried out administrative tasks, but soon I was assigned to patrols due to the lack of personnel. I gave my best effort and even initially found understanding from my comrades; however, when it came down to it, there were no changes. The mental blocks persisted. My limitations resurfaced during combat situations that could pose a risk to my comrades, so the medical team recommended I take an extended leave to recover.

I returned to the kibbutz, where I was warmly welcomed since they had stopped hiring Arab workers due to the rising tensions and were in need of labor. I began working at the trailer and agricultural machinery factory, where the lack of manpower was more acutely felt. Young people and fit adults were sent to the workshops, working forty-hour weeks, carrying heavy loads, and operating machinery that required skill and strength. We had become a true factory, and we no longer just sent trailers to other kibbutzim—we sold them across the country, and some were exported abroad. The changes that accompanied this successful source of income brought more specialization. Weekly rotations between the factory, the pear harvest, the dairy, or kitchen duties were no longer in place. Each member focused on tasks they were deemed most suited for.

The transformation of the kibbutz went further, and some means of production were privatized. Ownership of the trailer factory was shared with a company responsible for commercialization; the communal dining services had been outsourced, and many residents no longer used them. Differential salaries and private property were widely implemented. Some residents had even bought their homes, and though they still lived in the kibbutz, they commuted daily to Haifa for work. That idyllic society of the founders, partially inherited by my generation, persisted in the minds of nostalgic individuals like me, but it had evolved into an urban center teetering between a typical Western town and an individualistic American suburb. I suppose that's life, and we must adapt. It's of little use to console oneself by saying the past was better.

In the metallurgical factory, I was put in charge of the sheet metal section. We cut steel sheets to the specified dimensions and then stamped them, preparing them for assembly. The work was exhausting but gratifying. These two characteristics suited my recovery well. It was gratifying because, at the end of each day, I could see the newly built trailers lined up in front of the hangar. It was exhausting because the physical effort left me collapsing into bed, providing me with restful sleep. As time passed, I healed, and just as sediment settles in a cistern, leaving the water clear on the surface, my mind began to clarify, filtering through the thoughts that prevailed over the others.

The result of this process was far from what my army psychologists had hoped for, but it acquired the strength and perfection of a pearl, formed by the gradual deposition of fine layers of nacre. I stopped obsessing over the effect of the Palestinian marrow on my reasoning, but I continued to reinforce the idea that Jews and Palestinians must find a way to coexist. Fate had brought our two peoples, both wronged by others with whom they had coexisted throughout history, to share the same small and resource-limited territory. It was our responsibility to come to an agreement and find the best way to live together. Our method of colonizing the land was driven by urgency and the need to establish a population cruelly persecuted in Europe, accompanied by the intelligence and determination of people who knew how to transform barren land into fertile ground and create a modern society that enabled the full development of men and women. In our unstoppable progress, the Palestinian people had been displaced, and while efforts were initially made to accommodate them, they were gradually pushed into a corner where only despair remained. The great challenge we now faced in Israel was finding a way for Palestinians and Jews to live together in that land. Recently, the idea of creating two states had been discussed, and some even proposed a confederation with freedom of movement. I am not a politician, and I don't know what solution will eventually be implemented, but I am certain that dialogue is the only way for us to live in peace. Many enemies and agents of destabilization will arise, but if we manage to come to an agreement and remain steadfast, we will succeed. Chimeras are unstable and carry within themselves the seeds of reactions that can destroy them, but only continuous action to strengthen them will lead us to a just and lasting society. Finally, I had found the purpose of my life, a cause to which I could dedicate my efforts to keep fighting.

During a visit from an old kibbutz mate who worked for the government, we had a heated discussion over a long dinner and even longer after-dinner conversation. He understood my ideas and assured me that many people did, giving me a long list of authors and books to read and encouraging me to move to Jerusalem to meet others who shared my way of thinking.

"Yuval, we need people like you who want to join the peace movements," he said, his voice almost pleading. Then he lifted his head, and with a proud look continued. "There are many of us, and we have to support each other. Each of us contributes in our own way; together, we can find a peaceful solution."

I moved at the end of autumn, and thanks to his contacts, I began working at a busy government office. I've been doing all sorts of small support jobs, from IT documentation and propaganda assistance to security at some events, given my recent military experience. I'm what's called a "jack of all trades"—not indispensable, but I know that thanks to my help, many of the planned actions can go ahead.

It's now the end of January, and we've come to Taba for a summit between Israel and the Palestinian National Authority. My bosses are very pleased and say it's the peace conference where the most progress has been made. Representatives from both sides are interested in a solution, which they hope will later be approved by their respective governments. Israel will have elections in early February, and the outcome will be crucial for advancing the agreements. Many critical issues remain, including the return of Palestinian refugees, the status of Jerusalem, and control over Jewish settlements in the West Bank and Gaza. But at least they are talking and debating these issues instead of shooting at each other in open fields.

The night is mild, and I've come to the beach to listen to the sea and let myself be carried by the ebb and flow of the waves. The water is a deep blue, reflecting the lights of Aqaba in the distance. A few meters to my left is the border with Israel, and just a few kilometers further is the city of Eilat. So many dividing lines grouped in such a small territory. The good thing is that here, you feel like people have hope for improvement and that peace prevails.

The water caresses my feet in gentle movements, and I bend down to wet my hands in the calm surface of the sea. Lying on the sand, I stretch my arms out wide and move them up and down, leaving the outline of a human figure with extended wings drawn on the beach. I know it's a dream, a chimera. But as I stand up and see the winged figure reflecting the light of the crescent moon, I feel a shiver run through me, filling me with excitement and hope.

V

The death of the Chimera

The title of this chapter is contradictory because the Chimera is sempiternal—it had a beginning, but it has no end. It is immortal. In the Greek myth, the Chimera is killed by Bellerophon, who, riding the winged horse Pegasus, approaches her and thrusts a spear into her mouth. Due to the fire emanating from her throat, the lead tip of the spear melts, and this brings about her death. This battle has been depicted many times in both Greek and Roman ceramics and mosaics. Many of these representations aim to showcase Bellerophon's feat, but in all of them, the monster has a prominent presence, either because it heightens the hero's glory or because the beast's iconography is fascinating.

Bellerophon is a controversial character because, although he achieved several great feats, he was extremely arrogant. To give you an idea, after accidentally killing a tyrant of Corinth named Bellerus, he changed his original name to "Bellerophon," meaning "killer of Bellerus." For some authors, he personifies reason annihilating the perversions represented by the Chimera. Therefore, this represents a crushing kind of reason, one that assures us we possess the truth and feel entitled to impose it on others. Other authors highlight his insolent arrogance, which led him to attempt an ascent to Olympus on Pegasus to become a god. Zeus didn't bother much; he sent a mere mosquito, which, with a single sting on Pegasus' back, caused the horse to rear up, throwing Bellerophon to the ground, where he was injured. As punishment, Bellerophon was condemned to wander, crippled and isolated from the rest of the world for the rest of his life. Perhaps his ambition to annihilate chimerical perversions was already a sign of excess.

Pegasus, on the other hand, is a more attractive and less controversial myth. He was the son of Poseidon and was given to Bellerophon by Athena, either directly or through magical reins that allowed him to tame the horse. When he ascended to Olympus, Zeus kept him in his stables, where he became one of his favorite horses. The myth of the winged horse exists in many cultures, from Eastern to Arab traditions, and its representation has been incorporated into modern iconography.

It's curious that, while Pegasus represents strong ties to the myths of reason like Athena and Bellerophon, the figure also has a chimerical touch, as it unites two realities: the body of a horse and the wings of a bird. Perhaps it tells us that leaving room for the mysterious and the unknown within pure reason can have its advantages—among them, the humility of recognizing our own limitations.

It seems more fitting to forget Bellerophon and think of Pegasus as a representation of reason and intellect that doesn't seek death, but rather control over the Chimera—one that pursues imaginative exaltation to enhance the strength of rational myth. In fact, this interpretation could resolve the initial contradiction: The Chimera wasn't killed, but merely defeated, and now lies in hiding. According to some poets, she is desolate because she no longer has the power she once wielded, but who knows—with a little help, perhaps she could return. Maybe she could come back in gentler forms and enrich human life.

These gentler forms of the Chimera may come from Robert Graves's interpretation of the myth. In his view, the Chimera's defeat represents the dominance of patriarchal societies over the original matriarchal ones. Those ancient pantheistic societies, in which the Chimera represented the passage of life or time, were relegated and replaced by the new Greek theology, where a despotic and misogynistic Zeus wielded power and spread his seed at will. The Chimera's defeat closes the door on the previous myths and relegates them to the underworld and the forces of darkness. Thus, the way chimeras might return is by bringing back some of those primordial matriarchal forces that were once banished.

Another interesting aspect of the myth is how the Chimera dies. First, Bellerophon tries to kill her with arrows, but they do no harm. Then, he introduces a piece of lead into one of her mouths. In some versions, the lead is at the tip of a spear, while in others, it is a projectile swallowed by the monster. In any case, what's interesting is that the lead melts due to the fire within the beast, damaging her vital organs and causing her death. In other words, the enemy of the Chimera is inside her—her own strength and ferocity lead to her downfall.

It doesn't seem far-fetched to think that, to bring the myth into the present, we would need a good team of

doctors. A team capable of controlling the struggles between the Chimera's various components, giving her a
second chance to live.

The fight for life

Since ancient times, humans have been interested in re-using others' limbs to repair bodies with missing parts. It's easy to understand, as it's a very intuitive reaction: If a man loses an arm, the logical step would be to try and replace it with one from a companion or an enemy; if a woman loses the use of her hand in an accident, perhaps it could be replaced with a functional one. Reality, however, is stubborn, and early attempts would show that such grafts didn't work. A skilled shaman might succeed in reattaching a piece of ear or finger to the same body from which it had been severed, but joining parts from two different bodies was impossible. After much effort, modern medicine managed to unravel the mystery and understand why such unions were un-viable, accomplishing this step by step in a history we can call "the fight for life."

The idea of creating chimeras had already occurred to prehistoric humans. One of the earliest artistic expressions we know of, dated to around 32,000 years ago, features a human body with the head of a lion, found in the Stadel cave in Germany. Other prehistoric depictions show similar hybrid figures, most likely supported by the animist beliefs of our ancestors, which persisted for a long time. There are countless examples of such mixed representations throughout history, found in Assyrian, Egyptian, Hindu, or Chinese remains that spread in various forms to the Persian and Greco-Roman worlds. Even in Christian tradition, they were incorporated and passed into the modern world with great reverence—just think of Saints Cosmas and Damian, two physicians from the Arabian Peninsula who were canonized, one of their miracles being the grafting of a leg onto a deacon whose own had been amputated due to illness. But all of this was fiction, as transplants of limbs and organs between different bodies weren't attempted until the 19th century, and the first successes didn't come until well into the 20th century.

The biggest challenge to performing transplants was how to connect the grafted organ to the recipient's body. This was solved thanks to advances in vascularization made in the first decade of the 20th century by researchers like Frenchman Alexis Carrel. Originally from Lyon, his family came from the textile industry, and he had learned sewing techniques from some of the best French embroiderers. After graduating in medicine, he emigrated to the United States, where he joined pioneering teams in experimental surgery, specializing in organ and tissue transplant research. In the early 20th century, he proposed a method of vascular suturing that allowed blood vessels, veins, and arteries to be connected. Until then, they had been joined using bone or precious metal cannulas, which caused clots, thrombosis, and continuous failures. His new method closely resembled embroidery work: The surgeon would fold back the walls of the vessel ends and suture them with paraffin, much like hemming a sleeve. This method successfully connected the vessels, and no loose threads were left inside, avoiding previous problems. This was an essential first step in connecting and enabling different organs and tissues to function. A highly skilled surgeon, Carrel was able to join blood vessels just one millimeter in diameter, applying his technique to improve the success of autografts in animals and humans[10].

With the connection problem solved, the following decades saw numerous attempts to transplant organs between two different bodies, both between animals—mainly dogs—and between animals and humans. The surgeons of this era were astonishingly bold: Grafts were done by placing a kidney on a dog's back or hind leg, and a woman once had a goat's kidney grafted onto her elbow.

A single doctor performed more than 100 transplants between dogs. This suggests that suturing techniques were greatly refined, but it also implies that stray dogs most likely avoided hospitals equipped with the latest technology. All these transplants had one thing in common: They ended in failure. Within a few days, the animal or the patient—or both—died. Clearly, there was something beyond vascularization preventing the success of viable organisms.

Nevertheless, researchers were undeterred and continued their work, leading to several attempts at human kidney transplants by the mid-century. The kidney had become the organ of choice because it was relatively easy to graft, its function could be easily confirmed by urine production, and, obviously, the fact that each person has two kidneys increased the availability of organs from living donors. It was hoped that performing transplants between humans would mitigate the rejection problems associated with interspecies grafts. There were even transplants between close family members, such as a mother donating to her son, in the hope that kinship would facilitate compatibility. The most famous case occurred in 1952 when a 16-year-old French carpenter lost his only kidney in a work accident. His desperate mother volunteered to donate one of hers, and the team of Jean Hamburger agreed to perform the transplant to save the boy from his terminal condition. Unfortunately, despite initial success, the young carpenter died 22 days after the graft.

Other attempts followed, and some transplants functioned for weeks—months in the best cases—but most lasted only one or two days. The new discoveries underscored the key role of the immune system in the exchange between cells from different individuals. Austrian Karl Landsteiner had discovered blood groups, which had expanded the success of blood transfusions. In the lab, it was found that repeatedly breeding mice from the same lineage produced pure lines with very similar genetic makeups, and organ transplants between these individuals resulted in minimal rejection issues.

In fact, the first successful human transplant indirectly demonstrated the importance of immune compatibility, as it was performed between two identical twin brothers with identical genetics. On December 23, 1954, Dr. John Murray's team in Boston (U.S.) performed the procedure. One of the brothers, Richard Herrick, was diagnosed with kidney disease at 23 that would have killed him within months. His brother Ronald donated one of his healthy kidneys, and the surgery was a complete success. Richard survived and led an active life without rejection for the next eight years. He even married one of the nurses who cared for him and had several children before dying of causes unrelated to the transplant. His brother Ronald died 55 years after the operation, becoming the donor of the first successful transplant of a vital organ in human history.

This marked the beginning of a period when the experience gained with kidneys encouraged the expansion of transplants to other organs. In the early 1960s, the first human liver transplant was performed by Dr. Thomas Starzl, and the first lung transplant by Dr. James Hardy. These organs only lasted a little over two weeks, but they proved it was possible to graft these organs, and the next step was learning how to keep patients alive. In 1967, Dr. Barnard performed the first heart transplant in South Africa, which had a huge global impact and helped raise awareness of the potential of these techniques. The operation was broadcast worldwide, and surgeons were seen as true heroes fighting to save lives. The recipient was 56-year-old Louis Washkansky, terminally ill with heart failure, and the donor was 26-year-old Denise Darvall, who was brain-dead following a car accident. The operation lasted nine hours, and the patient was stable upon leaving the operating room, but he only survived for 18 days, a survival period similar to that of most liver and lung transplant patients. It was known that the widespread failure of these grafts was due to organ rejection, but the mechanism to control it was not yet understood.

In parallel with surgical advances in transplants, knowledge of the immune system expanded dramatically. In addition to blood groups, researchers discovered how the antigen–antibody complex worked, the origin of antibodies in plasma lymphocytes, and ultimately the HLA system—human leukocyte antigens. The HLA system is the genetic profile unique to each person, with half coming from each parent at conception, forming a new specific HLA genotype. It ensures the immune response to foreign agents in our body by recognizing the presence of cells with a different genetic makeup and activating the defense system, protecting us from infections or cancerous mutations. The discovery of the HLA system is credited to Dr. Jean Dausset and explained why transplants had only succeeded between identical twins: To avoid rejection, the organs had to be HLA-compatible. Given the complexity of the HLA system, the odds of success in grafting a foreign organ into a recipient's body were extremely low and could only be ensured through pre-selection.

These odds of compatibility were so low that they limited transplant success to exceptional cases, requiring either a highly sophisticated system for finding and matching organs or some way to weaken the recipient's immune system. The latter option emerged in the late 1970s with the discovery of cyclosporine, a drug that reduces the recipient's immune activity and lowers the risk of organ rejection. Swiss Sandoz laboratories had a program searching for antibiotics, in which they collected soil samples from around the world and isolated their microorganisms. From a sample of soil from Norway, they isolated a fungus capable of producing an unknown substance: cyclosporine. This compound had little value as an antibiotic, so it was discarded from the program, ending up almost by accident in the laboratory of immunologist Dr. Borel. Early experiments with rats showed cyclosporine's ability to inhibit antibody production, and in transplants between these animals, it proved ideal for mitigating rejection problems by suppressing the recipient's immune system. This breakthrough opened the door to the survival of transplant patients!

The development of immunosuppressive therapies to control rejection, combined with advances in complementary surgical techniques, led to a rapid increase in transplant success rates at the end of the last century, and the use of these modern medical techniques spread across much of the world during the 21st century. Today, this fight for life isn't completely won, as failed cases still occur and improvements are still needed, but it has allowed for memorable triumphs in the transplants of vital organs, including bone marrow transplants.

Historically, organ availability has always been a limitation for transplants, with a far higher number of patients in need of an organ than there are available donors. Until the late 1960s, organ exchange was primarily local and informal, but several key milestones changed the situation. The first organization for organ exchange is credited to Dr. Terasaki, who in 1967 created a donor registry in Los Angeles, California. Dr. Terasaki was a tireless worker specializing in immunological studies, developing international HLA characterization standards to add to the registry and facilitate finding compatible donors. Interestingly, as his family was of Japanese origin, he spent three years of his youth in an internment camp for Japanese-Americans in Arizona during World War II. It's fascinating to note how this experience didn't create bitterness in him toward the society that had restricted his freedom; instead, he contributed through an example of philanthropic generosity. The following year, a similar organ procurement organization was established in New England, and in the following years, other states and countries founded organ donation centers. Today, national transplant organizations and other foundations are doing excellent work both in raising awareness among the public about the importance of donating their organs to help save or improve the lives of others, and in coordinating exchanges between patients, regions, and countries. These organizations have made it possible to develop the sophisticated capture, characterization, and preservation system needed to increase the likelihood of finding HLA-compatible organs. Locating a compatible donor either in the patient's country or abroad, coordinating the organ's extraction in the morning to ensure its transportation, and then grafting it into the recipient in the afternoon is a feat comparable to many of the battles mythologized in absurd wars throughout history.

Another important milestone in organ transplants was the definition of the concept of brain death or encephalic death. This is attributed to French doctors Mollaret and Goulon, who questioned the meaning of death in terminal patients. They observed that some patients who entered an irreversible coma could never return because they had suffered a complete cessation of brain activity. In some cases, the functions of vital organs could be maintained, which understandably caused controversy at the time. The question was inevitable: When can a patient be declared dead? In 1968, a committee of experts from Harvard Medical School established the criteria for defining brain death, and in the following years, these criteria were incorporated into the legislation of Western countries. Once brain death was widely accepted, the door was opened for organs from such individuals—still functional and viable—to be donated to save the lives of others. Today, it's possible to make a living will, in which a person can specify that in the event of an accident or terminal illness, they wish to donate their organs to patients in need. If the terminally ill individual has not made such a will, the family can consent to the donation of their organs. Thanks to these donations, based on people's generosity, thousands of lives are saved each year around the world.

Despite all this, it's estimated that in Europe, for every nine people waiting for a transplant, there is only one donor available each year. This is why xenotransplantation offers an exciting option for increasing the availability of organs in the future. Xenotransplants are transplants of organs between different animal species, with those from pigs to humans currently showing the most promise. Experimental transplants of hearts and kidneys have already been successfully performed, and researchers are working to solve the problems of acute and hyperacute rejection that limit patient survival. These pigs are usually genetically modified, either through the introduction of human genes via transgenesis or through direct modification of their DNA. The modifications aim to increase the compatibility of the organs to be transplanted with human recipients, representing a scientific advance that could pose ethical dilemmas for some. However, we can overcome these prejudices if we think about the health benefits these new, properly regulated technologies can bring. A good way to understand this is to put ourselves in the shoes of others and imagine that the person in need of the transplant is a child, a sibling, or a loved one.

*   *   *

Bone marrow transplantation deserves a separate explanation to clarify misunderstandings. The marrow is located inside the bones, a very protected place where our blood is generated. Therefore, the transplant involves replacing the stem cells of the blood, also called hematopoietic cells, which means "blood creators" in Greek, with healthy stem cells. The majority of transplants performed are autologous, meaning the patient's own cells are extracted, treated outside their body, and then reintroduced once healthy. One-third are allogeneic transplants, where the stem cells injected into the patient come from a donor, making the transplanted organism a chimera. The goal is to change the entire immune system and blood-generating system of the patient, one of the most difficult biological challenges faced by medicine regarding transplants.

If there is a researcher who has stood out in the field of blood stem cell transplants, it is Dr. D.E. Thomas, who performed the first transplant in 1956. His team administered intravenous injections to six patients with terminal hematological diseases using bone marrow extracted from the interior of the ribs and iliac crests of a corpse, a fetus, and living adult donors. All the patients died shortly afterward, probably due to graft-versus-host disease, as the importance of the HLA system was still unknown, but it demonstrated that it was possible to repopulate and produce new marrow using this type of graft. In subsequent years, other attempts were made by various medical teams. For example, transplants were carried out to treat leukemias that appeared after exposure to high doses of radiation in victims of a nuclear accident, but no long-term survival was achieved in any case.

Hematologists joined oncologists in the search for immunosuppressive treatments to control rejection problems, while also advancing in improvements in transfusion equipment and treatments for infections. Thus, we arrived at 1969, when Dr. Thomas's team successfully performed the first transplant of stem cells from a donor to a recipient who was not an identical twin. In the last decades of the 20th century, advances in allogeneic grafts progressed spectacularly. By the early 21st century, they were extended for the treatment of cancerous diseases such as leukemias and lymphomas, as well as other blood diseases, in many countries around the world. Dr. Thomas received the Nobel Prize along with Dr. Murray in 1990 for their advances in transplant medicine. Despite not being a particularly wealthy person, he donated the entire $350,000 prize to the Fred Hutchison Cancer Center, where he had worked curing patients for much of his life.

You may be wondering how the bone marrow graft is performed. Currently, there are three methods: direct graft of bone marrow, through peripheral blood, or via umbilical cord blood. The first involves the direct absorption of the donor's bone marrow, which will be transplanted into the recipient. This is performed in the operating room with general or epidural anesthesia for the donor, who undergoes punctures in the bones and has their bone marrow aspirated, which is then grafted into the recipient. Today, this technique has been reduced to very few cases, fortunately for donors as they do not have to undergo such a complicated operation.

The most commonly used technique is the extraction via peripheral blood, in which the donor receives daily subcutaneous injections for the five days prior to the extraction, thereby stimulating the production of stem cells that are released into the blood. On the fifth day, blood is drawn with a catheter, passing it through a machine that separates the stem cells from the rest through centrifugation and membranes. The donor's own blood is then returned to their body via the same catheter. This process is called apheresis and can last between four and six hours, depending on the quantity of stem cells required, and it minimizes discomfort for the donor. It is normal for them to experience some fatigue, but they recover in a few days and no side effects have been detected. The harvested stem cells are injected into the recipient through a catheter, a process that is not associated with any pain, and the recipient is prepared to undergo suffering related to the elimination of their toxic bone marrow through chemotherapy or radiotherapy, along with the graft-versus-host disease that can last between six months and a year, in most cases.

Minimizing the discomfort suffered by the donor is highly relevant since, although the techniques were designed to save many lives, there was still one fundamental piece missing. How to find an HLA-compatible bone marrow donor? In 1971, Shirley Nolan, an English secondary school teacher who had emigrated to Australia, gave birth to a boy, Anthony Nolan, who was diagnosed with a rare blood disease called Wiskott–Aldrich syndrome. The only solution to prolong his life was to replace his bone marrow through a transplant. After studying close family members, none were found to be

HLA compatible, so his mother launched an international campaign to find a potential donor. She did not succeed, just as three-quarters of needy patients do not, and her son died at the age of seven. It must have been very hard for Shirley, but what is admirable is her reaction. In 1974, filled with courage, she founded the first bone marrow donor registry in the UK, which is now part of the Anthony Nolan Foundation. It has helped save many lives and served as an example to many other countries. In Spain, a similar registry was founded in 1988 by tenor Josep Carreras after he suffered from leukemia. In Europe, all registries are coordinated, and in 2008, a milestone was achieved with more than half of the bone marrow donors being non-relatives of the recipients.

Thanks to all these advances, "leukemia has changed from being a disease that a few decades ago was a death sentence," in the words of Dr. Thomas, to having a survival rate over 70%, according to data provided by the Josep Carreras Foundation[11]. The journey in the fight for life has been long, and there is still a good way to go.

VI

Gratitude and generosity

The entire fight for life that so many doctors and researchers have dedicated their careers to has an epic character, so much so that Homer could well come to compose odes to all the heroes who have participated in it. My tribute aims to be more modest, but it would be incomplete if I did not include recognition for all the healthcare teams around the world involved in the transplant processes. As I believe that the best way to generalize this is to start from the concrete, I want to express my deepest gratitude to the staff of the hospital where I was admitted and who provided me with the necessary care to move forward: the Fundación Jiménez Díaz in Madrid.

I entered the hospital by chance. A blood test for some unimportant preoperative tests revealed that I had acute myeloid leukemia. I was told that I was alive by chance; I could have dropped dead at any moment in the street from a cardiac arrest, and I was urgently admitted to undergo treatment to control the disease. Two chemotherapies, a first called induction and a second consolidation, allowed cancer cell levels to drop below four percent after two and a half months. At those levels, it is considered that the disease does not cause further damage, but depending on the aggressiveness of the leukemia, it is not possible to guarantee that there will not be a new outbreak in the following months. While the treatment lasted, the medical team conducted studies to assess the severity of the disease. In my case, it had not spread to the rest of my body, and the leukemia was classified as having intermediate aggressiveness. Had it been highly aggressive, I probably would have succumbed before writing this text. It was also clear that it was not mild, as evidenced by the symptoms and the difficulty in controlling it. The solution lay in a bone marrow transplant to replace my current marrow with a healthy one capable of producing functional blood.

During this entire time, I was in the hands of the hospital's healthcare team, first isolated in a room during the month-long induction chemotherapy, and later with shorter admissions of a week or just outpatient visits to continue the therapy. When a person is subjected to such aggressive treatments, the first thing they feel is that they lose control of their body. Nausea prevents eating and drinking normally, causing uncontrollable vomiting that comes from the depths of your insides. You lose taste and appetite; sores develop in your mouth and throat that make swallowing difficult, and ingesting food to maintain your strength becomes a torment. The digestive system acts independently, causing endless diarrhea that expels what little you have been able to ingest with so much effort. How many hours did I spend sitting on the toilet in the middle of the night to avoid putting on the diapers that eventually became inevitable! The process is accompanied by weight loss and muscle mass, along with the loss of all body hair and the appearance of rashes or hives on the skin. In summary, not only do you lose control of your organism, but you also stop recognizing yourself in your own body; you are even surprised when you enter the bathroom and see that skeletal bald figure reflected in the mirror, resembling someone from a concentration camp. However, I will not dwell on the material misery; I prefer to recognize the merits of the healthcare professionals who helped me overcome this situation and enabled my mind to maintain vitality and optimism.

Nurses and aides caring for me tirelessly. Day and night, replacing IV fluids and medications, serving food that was scarcely eaten, attending to my complaints when the pain intensified. They were responsible for taking blood samples and performing dressings, always with good humor and encouraging words.

I remember one time, at four in the morning, when they had to draw blood from the catheter to monitor a septicemia that had developed and was causing periodic fevers. There was no way for blood to come out through the catheter lines; both were blocked. The nurse washed the capillaries with saline and repeatedly tried to aspirate with a syringe. The light from the headboard reflected the beads of sweat forming on her forehead. She kept insisting without success but did not waver. She asked me to sit up to see if that way more blood would come out; we managed small advances by moving, so I ended up doing sit-ups in the early morning to fill the two test tubes that were required. One hour of the clock was dedicated to drawing the sample, all the while giving me encouragement to not lose hope. When her shift ended at six-thirty, she came to say good morning and take my temperature before saying goodbye. Some experiences bond people forever, although I have probably become just another patient she has assisted diligently.

On another occasion, I woke up in the middle of the night with intense abdominal pain. I tried to get out of bed to go to the bathroom but couldn't. Those were the days when I was weaker, lacking the physical strength to move; my spirits were low after a few days of high fevers. Before I could help it, I found myself surrounded by feces, wet with my urine. An unpleasant feeling invaded my mind; I felt ashamed of myself for being unable to control my body. It was a humiliating situation. Making an effort, I rang the nurse's bell; a young aide, around twenty-two or twenty-three years old, came. When she saw the state I was in and the pitiful look on my face, she spoke to me kindly and firmly, telling me what I had to do without making me feel like she was ordering me around. She asked me to turn to one side and hold on to the bed's protective railing, keeping my body resting on my side. I obediently complied as she continued speaking calmly and first cleaned the mattress, then the sheets, and finally my soiled body. Then it was time for the other side; we repeated the procedure, and she removed all the dirty bedding to let me roll over onto the clean sheets placed on the mattress in the previous maneuver. My frail body was exposed, naked but now clean, and she took my arm and put it around her neck to help me into a hospital gown first and a diaper afterward. The aide kept talking just to make me feel good, praising how well I was cooperating, downplaying her work. I lay down, relaxed between the fresh, clean sheets, and when I thanked her for doing such a great job, she kindly said, "That's our job; we are here to help." She left the room, turning off the light behind her; I closed my eyes, and for the rest of the night, I slept like a baby.

Men and women who dedicate their time to helping others; I am grateful not only because their care has been essential for me to emerge successfully from this situation, but because they also make you feel that humanity is worth it. Although there are countless atrocities committed by human beings that we hear about daily through the news, there are people capable of devoting themselves to assisting and helping others in the most difficult moments. My sincerest gratitude goes to all of them.

And I do not want to miss the opportunity to recognize the work of the cleaning staff. Every day, they disinfected the room, changed the sheets, and provided clean pajamas and changes of clothes. Not to mention those who behind the scenes washed and sterilized the fabrics, prepared the food, and allowed the hospital to function. I got to know the cleaning staff personally, Isa and Cristina; I was not lucky enough to see those who worked behind the scenes, so I also send my recognition to them from here.

I have a good anecdote regarding the cleaning staff. During the first period of isolation that followed the induction chemotherapy, the general elections in Spain were held in July 2023. I asked the doctors how I should proceed to request a mail-in ballot from the hospital to be able to vote. They did not know, so they consulted their colleagues and the next day they explained to me how to do it: I had to arrange for a notary to come to the hospital to formalize the request for the mail-in vote and hand him the envelope with the ballot in my room. It seemed very complicated, and I gave up, feeling somewhat disappointed. On the deadline for requesting the mail-in vote, Isa, the cleaning staff, asked me if I was going to vote in the upcoming elections. I explained to her that I would not because it was too complicated and that I did not know any notary I could trust to ask them to come to the clinic. She then told me that before working in cleaning, she had worked in the hospital's postal services and that organizing mail-in voting was very easy. A notary passed through all hospital units, and one only had to express the desire to vote while identifying themselves with an ID card. He would facilitate the request for patients who needed it and then collect the ballots. Sure enough, it could not have been easier. This shows that questions should be asked of the right people. The cleaning staff member had the answer for mail-in voting, a competence as important as maintaining hygiene, without which neither society nor the hospital could function properly. How important are base-level positions, and how little do we appreciate them in our daily lives!

Let this comment not be interpreted to detract from the medical team, whom I deeply admire and owe my life to. Their early detection of the disease opened the opportunity to control it before it caused further damage to other organs, and the medical team made sure to take advantage of the gap that chance had revealed. From the beginning of my hospital admission, they started with the analyses; in parallel, they examined all my organs to assess the extent and severity of the disease, studied the genetic mutations of the cancer cells to personalize the treatment, and conducted a compatibility study of my siblings' bone marrow. It turned out that my younger sister was completely compatible, and alongside the results obtained in the rest of the tests, it allowed the doctors to compile a detailed report on my situation, which was approved by the regional transplant committee ten weeks after I was admitted.

It is noteworthy how empathetic the doctors are with the patient; in large hospitals, it seems that doctors are unreachable characters with whom one has brief contact during the morning rounds. My experience showed me doctors who were always attentive to my needs and feelings. When the transplant was approved, they explained in detail what it would entail and the risks I would be exposed to. I had two immediate reactions: to go sign my will right after leaving the meeting—better to have the legal situation well organized!—and to request permission to spend four days with my wife and daughters near the sea. I had spent two and a half months of summer unable to leave Madrid, more than half of the time confined to a clinical room. The doctor immediately understood my feelings, gave me all possible support, and organized my short discharge and readmission to accommodate my request. The four of us traveled to the ocean, and I cherished the wonderful sunsets of the Oyambre natural park, a great help for the next confinement.

Upon returning from the trip, the bone marrow transplant process began, which would lead to my healing. Isolation for a month in a pressurized room to avoid infections, undergoing conditioning chemotherapy to prepare the body for the transplant. The term "conditioning," a euphemism for complete disorder, involves killing the original bone cells so they can be replaced by the donor's new cells. The body's defenses are brought to a minimum, and all the ailments that appeared during the first chemotherapies reappear multiplied and combined with some new ones. The body weakens severely, the pains intensify, the journey is deep, and morphine becomes a good companion. It is difficult to get out of bed, and when you manage to do so to prevent bedsores or lung congestion, you feel cramps in your legs and can hardly walk.

Throughout this time, the doctors adjust the treatment to each patient's particular conditions; the medication and intravenous nutrition are tailored to personal needs to avoid exceeding the limits of what is intolerable. In this way, little by little, step by step, you gradually regain enough control of your body to be sent home. There is still a long process supervised by the doctors until you are discharged; complications and rejections arise during the transplant consolidation, but now with the feeling that the most challenging moments are behind you.

The final result of this process is a medical chimera, in which the donor's marrow and blood coexist with the recipient's organism. In my case, since my sister is the donor, it means that the blood cells with XX chromosomal loading coexist with the rest of my body, which is XY. This type of chimera falls into those that began to appear at the end of the twentieth century; they are two human realities coexisting in the same organism, and it has been during the current century that medical science has managed to understand their complexity and make them viable.

When we talk about medical science, we must include everyone from the grassroots researchers in their laboratories taking the first steps and testing initial hypotheses to the team of doctors who ultimately apply the procedures to patients. They represent the intelligence and rationality that help our society—the best of humanity, which, through science, is able to discover our diseases and cure them to allow us to be reborn.

*   *   *

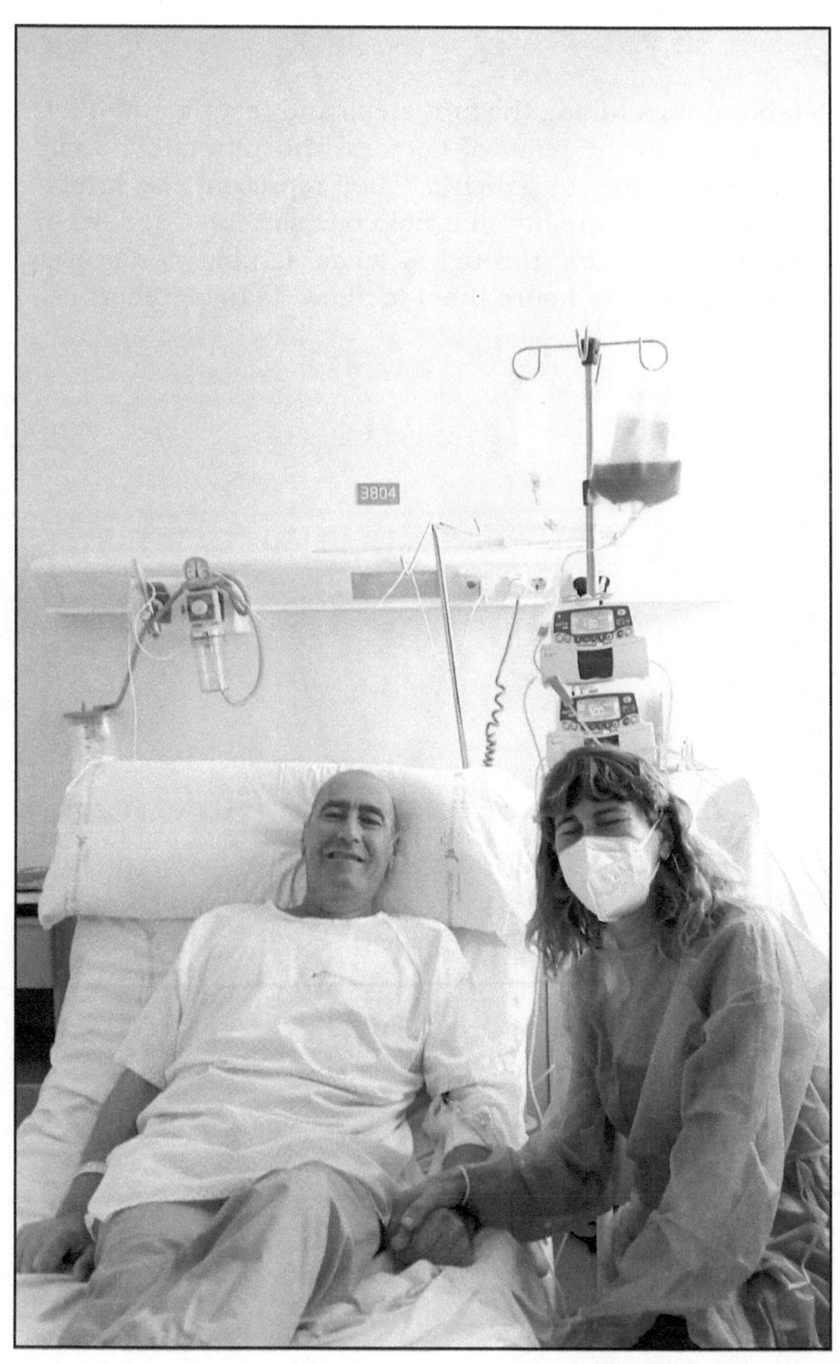

Dear María,

In the only image we have from the moment of the transplant, we appear together, our eyes almost closed, holding hands. You are wearing a mask, and behind us hangs a red bag from a metal pole above two infusion pumps. You are covered in a semi-transparent blue hospital wrapper, and I am wearing a white dotted gown that covers the edge of green pajama pants. At first glance, it doesn't seem special; even the quality of the photograph leaves a lot to be desired. However, it is a decisive moment in my life, and I know it is for you too.

Looking closely, one can see that the numbers "3804" appear above the head of the bed; we are in the fourth room of the clinical bubble designated for hematopoietic transplants at the Fundación Jiménez Díaz.

The red bag contains the stem cells that were extracted from you during the morning, and at the precise moment the image was captured by the hematologist, they are being injected into my body through the catheter in my left forearm. Those cells are yours; they are part of you, and they are being implanted into my body to take root inside my bones and replace my toxic marrow. The transplant lasts twenty minutes, and it is not a painful process at all. Physically, I feel nothing, but it is charged with emotion, as it is your donated cells that will allow me to survive.

If our eyes are closed, it is from having cried like babies; even the doctor and the nurse were moved. They were large, thick tears, the kind that leave your eyes wet and your vision blurred, as if we had so many feelings inside that they needed to burst forth through our eyes. I said, "Thank you, María," in a choked voice, and we exchanged a few phrases that I cannot remember; these are such emotional moments that there seems to be no room for words.

You hold my hand tenderly, and I still feel the warmth of your touch as if it were the moment captured in the photo. I had been isolated in the room for a week, undergoing chemotherapy to kill my marrow and make room for yours. During that time, I had not touched anyone; I had not felt the contact of another person. Your hands had been disinfected before entering the room, and yet that physical closeness was not medically advisable. But feeling our hands joined conveyed the warmth and affection I needed at that moment. The white and bright light of the early Madrid autumn floods through the side window, illuminating the room as if announcing that it brings life and that the transplant will work well—it will be a success.

The bag gradually emptied of red liquid; you left me alone in the room again, and as you departed, you encouraged me while shedding a tear or two. Now came the most challenging part for me, where the physical suffering became more intense, but I had held onto the warmth of your hand and that image stored on my phone. I looked at it gratefully to recharge my strength, to regain the energy necessary for this rebirth that you had gifted me.

You have always been overwhelmingly generous, almost difficult to comprehend. You have fallen in love with boys whom you helped with all your energies. You have taken in dogs—or rather, mutts—in need of care. Finally, you adopted your daughter because you wanted to be a mother, and you have dedicated yourself to her in a complete act of love through her education and your affection. Your generosity is so immense that at times it seems you need it to reaffirm yourself, to be who you are. It makes one want to tell you: "Be a little more selfish, take care of yourself, there's no need to save anyone else; you have already more than fulfilled your good deeds." Who knows where this need to help others comes from, perhaps from that complicated family we have had. It doesn't matter; it is beside the point. What is relevant is that it has led to what you call "a neurosis to save," a need to be the savior of people and animals. Now fate has given you the real opportunity to save a life—mine. It is not a neurosis; it is not a fiction. It is the unavoidable law of genetics that makes you my only close relative who is 100% HLA compatible.

I imagine the responsibility this entails for you. Suddenly, you are told that your brother needs a transplant of your marrow to survive. Inside your body exists something of immense value for another person, something irreplaceable that can give life to another human being. You told me that you were willing to do anything to take care of yourself, eat red meat if necessary to strengthen your marrow, give up your end-of-day cigarette, abandon yerba mate. It turned out that the tests they did showed you were in perfect health; you didn't have to change any of your habits, you just needed to continue as you had been. A great argument to defend your vegetarian diet and the stress-free life you decided to embrace with determination when you adopted Nabia. You left Madrid, its traffic, its pollution, its life of challenges and rush, to live near the sea in Tarifa, where you could lead a relaxed life that allowed you to take care of yourself and your daughter. What a surprise to discover that at the same time, you were safeguarding a part of yourself that would be so important for me. Unbeknownst to you, you were also preserving my life. As we have joked before, maybe after the transplant I will carry some of your alternative style with me, dedicating myself to a hippie life and contemplative meditation.

It was necessary to explain to Nabia that for a week, she would have to share her mother; moreover, she would stay in Tarifa attending school while you came to Madrid to receive the injections and undergo the transplant treatment. She was twelve years old, old enough to understand, but I know it was a great effort for both of you, always so close. So, thank you to your daughter as well, and please give her a big hug from me.

You told me that the five days spent in Madrid leading up to the transplant were very pleasant and that you enjoyed them a lot. Bright early autumn days when the temperature was perfect, inviting you to stroll through the city, to remember the places where you lived for so many years, to visit the friends who care about you so much. Before leaving home, you would give yourself a subcutaneous injection in the morning to stimulate the production of stem cells from your bone marrow, and then you had all day to do what you wanted. To continue taking care of yourself, to be calm, and to concentrate on ensuring that everything went well.

When the big day arrived, you were informed that it might need to be done in two sessions, as there was a significant weight difference between us, nearly 40 kilos. This isn't a time to offend me, but I think they slightly exaggerated my weight, estimating it at 91 kilos when I was actually at 80. We'll let that pass and focus on what we are talking about, but I just want to say that I wasn't overweight—perhaps a slight excess, but nothing more.

Early in the morning, they installed the catheter in your jugular, which isn't a pleasant experience for anyone, and you were settled into those reclining chairs they have at the blood bank. They are comfortable when you go in for an extraction that lasts ten or twenty minutes, but you had to sit there for six hours without moving. As you told me, you brought your relaxing alpha and beta wave music to listen to on your headphones while talking to your stem cells, urging them to come into the blood and do a good job. They connected you to the apheresis machine, and blood began to circulate; it flowed through the catheter, passed through the machine, the stem cells were removed, and the blood returned to your body. The doctors monitored the quantity of cells being produced; they were abundant and of good quality. You remained there stoically lying down; two friends even came to visit you to cheer you up and bring you something to eat. After four hours, the doctors gave you two options: to stop and continue the next day or to endure two more hours to collect the total number of cells needed. Being the brave person you are, you did not hesitate; it was better to continue until you had all the cells for the transplant. I was waiting upstairs in the room for the transplant, and you didn't want to keep me waiting.

By the way, the total number of cells is calculated based on the weight of the receiver, and in this case, about sixteen million cells were needed, which sounds like a lot. The little red bag hanging from the pole in the photograph, insignificant at first glance, contains that enormous sum of your cells that will be injected into me. The last hours were difficult; you found it hard to find a comfortable position on the chair, you felt pain in your hip and sacrum—more like pressure, as if your cells were pushing out from that point.

By early afternoon, the six hours had passed, and they disconnected you from the machine for checks. You had a forty-minute break in which you went outside the hospital to rest; they were going to call you at five o'clock to tell you if everything had gone well. I can imagine you exhausted after the whole process, wanting to feel satisfied but still uncertain about whether you had met the goal. The tranquility came punctually, and at five, they called you to say you had produced enough cells of excellent quality and that in half an hour, you were authorized to enter my room in unit 38 to assist in the transplant, just as I had requested.

It is the moment captured in the photograph. Tired and emotional, you give me your hand to transmit your strength and energy. You are happy to be able to give me the gift of life, and generously, you feel lucky to be the sister who can grant it. You told me that after going to bed that night, you slept for thirty hours straight when you got home. You woke up at six in the morning, leaving a day in between. Once you were up, you made a two-egg omelet and a mate of Argentine yerba; you had them to replenish your energy, filled with great satisfaction. Now it was time for your transplanted cells to do their work; you thought about them, encouraging them to combat my cancer but without harming me too much. In the hospital, you had left me isolated in a room of barely twenty square meters, but with a part of you inside me that would accompany me through the rest of my battle and my days.

Lying in bed with my eyes closed, I see the beach of Punta Paloma; it stretches long and drawn out as far as the eye can see. It is difficult to know if the arc of sand is drawn circling the sea or if it is the sea, in its tireless push, that is engulfing the sandy beach. The faint line that separates the water and the sand blurs due to the effect of the waves crashing on the shore and the whirlpools raised by the west wind. The morning light of Cádiz reflects on the ocean, a deep blue brought from the center of the Atlantic, and reverberates on the dry sand of the beach.

On the shoreline, I see you walking slowly, lazily, following the arc of the wet sand. Your dog, with a slight limp, runs back and forth, moving at the same pace set by her owner. I still have to find out if there is something of your essence that has come with me alongside your marrow. If so, I hope I have brought with me a bit of your bold decision to choose an alternative way to face life and, above all, some of your enormous generosity.

Thank you, María.

VII

Monologue

I'm a bit fed up with this bald guy, complaining all day, making demands, and now he comes up with moral stories, like we need to raise the heating because I've lost body fat and I'm very cold... well, just wait for the gas bill that's going to hit us this winter! and he wants to run a laundry just for himself to avoid cross-infections... crossed will be our bank account when the electricity bill comes, seems like he doesn't realize how much all this costs! or taking a taxi because he's so tired after our walk... what a gentleman! he thinks instead of getting cancer, he hit the lottery! seriously, what a time to have married this guy, a pretty face, lots of smiles, and a body that looked just fine, but when push came to shove, he didn't last the first blow, he hasn't even hit sixty, and he's already falling apart with all sorts of ailments, like I said, a flashy exterior but poor-quality interior, I already knew it, and I was warned, his parents died young, and his father, in particular, was disabled by a stroke soon after turning sixty, that already told me he wasn't built for endurance, but no matter how you slice it, genetics play a huge role in these things, look at me, a good Andalusian woman built like God intended, wide hips to have healthy children, and I've seen the doctor less than a wild partridge sees a vet, and then he tells me that what he suffers has nothing to do with his father, that his dad had a stroke, and he's got leukemia, thirty-five percent of cancerous cells in his blood! can you be more rotten inside? it's unbelievable! and the guy was riding his bike to work like nothing, stopped by the hospital for a blood test, and when they called him at noon to come straight to the ER, he cycled up the steepest hill in Madrid from the Manzanares River to the hospital, I don't know how he didn't collapse right there from a heart attack, heatstroke, or a cardiac arrest, he calls me from the ER around five in the afternoon telling me to come when I can, "when I can," he says, on a Monday in June when I'm buried in work up to my ears! I arrived at the ER around seven-thirty, they didn't make me wait long, but when I got there, I found a meeting with the hematologist on duty, and he drops the bomb, there's no other word for it, a bomb, he says it's a miracle he's still alive, that they need to give him a blood transfusion immediately to bring his hemoglobin to a level that'll keep him alive, that he can't even go home to get pajamas... he'll stay in the ER until they can find him a room upstairs, probably later tonight, and it's still too early for a definitive diagnosis, but we should be thinking of a year for his recovery, that's if all goes well... I was turning white; what a mess was about to befall us, and there he was with his sorry face, all "I didn't do anything," but oh, the storm we were about to face, and of course, I was the one who had to go and untie his bike from the hospital gate, I'm not saying it's his fault, the poor guy didn't do anything wrong, his little excesses of wine and beer here and there, but nothing worse than what everyone else does, he doesn't even smoke, he used to smoke when he was younger but quit when our daughters were born, we agreed to quit together, and that was over twenty years ago, I've smoked a cigarette or two on nights out or after a nice dinner, but him, not a single one, once, he tried taking a puff, and he started coughing like an old man, so yeah, he quit for good, and now he gets this, as I said, not his fault, but still, I was the one who had to collect the bike and take it home, I can't even ride it; it's as tall as a horse and heavy as a motorcycle, like I said, my darling husband has a flashy exterior, but when it comes down to it, he hasn't been much use, they moved him upstairs to oncology at three in the morning, and I don't need to tell you what that ward feels like, all the patients there have very serious problems, if it's not lymphoma, it's sarcoma, if someone doesn't have a tumor in one organ, it's because they have it in two or three, or who knows how many, one guy in the room next to us went home on palliative care because after three years of fighting, he was worse off than when he started, another one we shared a room with for a few days had a bacterial lung infection that forced him to stop all his cancer treatment, and after six months, he was back to square one, starting over, complete change of plans, and he caught the infection in the hospital, breathing in what's supposed to be filtered air to avoid diseases, but if you're stuck inside, it can't be good, the air you need is from the mountains, fresh and clean, even the doctors know that and send you home as soon as they see you can take care of yourself, they're the first ones who are afraid you'll catch some rare bug while you're in the hospital, especially in oncology, where there are so many strange diseases, it's a wonder anyone walks out of there on their own two feet, what a place! it's almost better not to talk much with the relatives of the other patients, and thank God there weren't any kids there because I couldn't have handled it, I just can't bear to see them suffer, they break my heart, I know they're the ones who fight the hardest and are an example to follow, but it's so hard to see them suffer through such a horrible illness, they didn't ask for it, but all of a sudden, they have to go through this terrible disease, I just wonder, this surely must shape their character because the innocence of childhood, the laughing and playing, just disappears, and suddenly they have to deal with all these worries, it's so difficult, really, just seeing the young adults in the ward gave me chills, thirty years old and having cancer in their prime, something that will limit them forever, life is so unfair, you get what you get, and you just have to deal with it and move forward, attitude is everything, sure, there were patients who were always complaining, but what did they gain from that? nothing, absolutely nothing, the best you can do is put on a brave face and push through whatever comes your way, follow what they tell you, and keep a good mood as much as possible, I know it's easier said than done, but it's the only option, and that's that, on the same floor, there were people from the cancer support association, such wonderful people! they came to offer their services for free: psychological support, psychiatric care, and even home help, it's such a big help for so many people who are stuck in there or have to continue their treatment from home, it's a whole world you discover when you're on the oncology floor, luckily or unluckily, for us, after four days they moved him into isolation, gave him a heavy dose of chemotherapy for a week, and then thirty days alone in a room, he had his own bathroom, at least, because they had taken his immune system down to zero, and it wasn't just his immune system, the poor guy was left a complete mess, he lost weight until he looked like a skeleton, bald as a billiard ball, vomiting, nausea, fevers, diarrhea... even his smell changed, I know his smell well, deep like a man from the woods, and it's not unpleasant, on the contrary, I like it, it's unmistakable, it clings to his clothes, his pajamas, I'd recognize it anywhere, blindfold me, and I could pick him out from a crowd in a minute, well, his smell changed, first, it started fading as his body hair fell out, and then it completely transformed overnight, they gave him chemotherapy that came out through his skin, they injected it through the catheter into his blood, and then he sweat it out through his pores, he had to shower after a few hours to wash away all the toxins he was sweating out, that's when his smell changed completely, and he never got it back, now he has this sour smell, like he's too clean, although his urine smells really strong, probably because of all the medication he's taking, a bunch of pills every day, and it all has to come out somehow, so I've had to forget his old smell and get used to the new one, that's just how it is, he also says that his taste has changed, he lost it in the hospital, which isn't surprising considering the food they served him, it wasn't bad, but it was bland and unappetizing, well, okay, it was bad, for a hospital, it could have been worse, but as food? it wasn't good, it might have been healthy for him, but it wasn't enjoyable, and I won't criticize more because, honestly, the hospital treated us great in every other way, so, for meals, stick to home; for healing, go to the hospital, but back to the taste issue, it faded away slowly because in the first few weeks, he was still enjoying the chocolates and treats people brought him, then he started saying he had a metallic taste in his mouth, and that's when he stopped enjoying food, he couldn't taste anything, neither the sweets nor the meals, eventually, he stopped eating, so he lost even more weight and turned into a string bean, for someone who loves to eat and drink good wine, my husband, the foodie, was suddenly left with nothing, one less pleasure in life, but at least it's not too bad, no, he says he's slowly getting his taste back, he's back in the kitchen preparing his little dishes and appreciating the flavors again, if only all his problems were like that! I used to visit him at the end of the day, they made me wear a sterile gown, a cap, and those hospital green shoe covers that make your teeth ache just thinking about them, and there I went, listening to the little he had to say and the long list of things he wanted, "this," "that," arguments over silly things, he even counted the tiles in the room, fifteen by ten, and made me bring a tape measure so he could measure them! according to him, each tile was forty centimeters square, so the room was twenty-four square meters, well, he measured them, and yep, he was right, I had said they were bigger, so he won! oh, how happy he was! well, let him be happy because I wasn't about to argue over something so silly, I left him there, locked up in his twenty-four square meters, one square meter for every hour of the day, I hadn't realized this, but that's what it came down to, he was supposed to exercise for his recovery, to prevent fluid from building up in his lungs, stop losing muscle mass, and who knows what else, so there he was, pacing the room back and forth to rack up the kilometers, like a hamster on a wheel, up and down, up and down, and I almost forgot, he had internal bleeding in his knee from low platelets, combined with early arthritis, so he was hobbling around on crutches, I cheered him on a lot, but honestly, it was pathetic, and if he was having a bad day, he'd be in such a foul mood that all I wanted to do was get out of there, better to remember the good days, and there were some of those too, on those days, we'd play board games I had bought, beautiful, by the way, wooden, very pleasant to the touch, and in lovely, muted colors, we started with checkers, but he always won, the sneaky guy, he'd been playing since he was a kid and knew all the tricks, so I dug around and found a backgammon set, which he didn't know how to play, we'd play, and I'd win every time! there was no way I was going to let him win with all his handicaps! well, maybe I'd let him win once or twice to lift his spirits a little, over time, he started eating a little more, and using the excuse that he needed to regain his sense of taste, honestly, he was so hung up on this taste issue, like there wasn't anything more important than eating and drinking! "hold on a bit, man, you'll get it back soon enough, and it won't be such a big deal," I thought, but anyway, he managed to convince me to bring him some muffins from a Galician bakery between our house and the hospital, he wasn't allowed to have food in his room, but he figured out how to hide them in the drawer of the bedside table, eating one for breakfast and another for a snack, I would bring him batches of six, so every three days I was his muffin mule! can you believe the trouble he gets me into? I don't even know how I agreed to it, why didn't I just tell him to eat the dry cookies they gave him? they're probably good for him! But seeing him in such bad shape, I figured I had to give in to some indulgence, look, I've always thought that men are such complainers, I'd love to see them give birth to a child—that's real suffering! but I have to admit, this chemotherapy stuff leaves some of the most awful side effects, It's a whole different thing than childbirth; you can't compare apples to oranges, there were days he really suffered, and on top of it all, there's the uncertainty of not knowing what will happen, like, what if things get worse, and it all goes downhill like it did with those other patients we shared the room with? knock on wood! It feels like a lottery, and you keep your fingers crossed, hoping everything will turn out okay, we already had enough to deal with because of this leukemia, let alone something even worse coming along, I found myself thinking, "If something worse happens, just let it be quick, take him fast, but without suffering he's been through enough," little by little, he started to recover, and even though it was a mystery where he found the strength, he kept at it, it was like watching a little kid at the beach, just when you think they're going to drown, they kick with their arms and legs, somehow keeping their head above water, not even knowing how they're doing it, but they keep going until they make it to shore, that's exactly what it was like in his case: some days he was up, some days he was down, but when it seemed like he couldn't go on anymore, he'd poke his nose up, gather strength, and start fighting again, most nights, I'd leave him there in bed, feeling heavy-hearted, he was stuck in that fishbowl, fighting his own battle, and there wasn't much I could do to help him except keep him company, looking back now, I feel proud of him, though I don't tell him because he already gets enough compliments from his friends, they all look at him with those tender eyes, because that's the thing, he looks so fragile, so pitiful, that you can't help but feel sympathy for him, he's the kind of person who just brings out your tenderness right away, I'm not going to be hard on him, because it's not in my heart, but I'm not going to be overly soft either, I'm not made of mush, but we got through that first hospital phase, and even though they sent him home all worn out, it was such a joy to have him back home, well, they only let him out for a week to regain some strength before sending him back into the pit, but still, having him home felt like a small victory, luckily, the second time they sent him back to the hospital, it was more bearable, he handled the chemo much better, and after ten days, they discharged him to continue his recovery at home, just thinking about it makes me shudder, couldn't they have kept him for another month? I'd have gone to visit him, beat him at backgammon, brought him muffins, and given him a kiss for a good night's sleep, but no, they sent him home for me to play head nurse again, patience, I had to stock up on patience, making his meals, even though I knew half of them would come right back up, now that was a real chimera spitting fire from its mouth, not the mythical battles he imagines with chimerism or whatever else, those vomits were real and fierce, and every time I saw his little bird-like face looking scared, I knew I had to brace myself for the worst, patience, that's what I had, because there wasn't much reward in it, as for anything sexual, let's not even mention it, he'd been completely drained, in every sense, let's just say he got affectionate in a child-like way, through tearful eyes, just like they do in soap operas, so, I'd soften up and keep pushing through the situation, but after the second round of chemo, he came out with even more cancer cells than after the first, and it was clear that the leukemia wasn't going anywhere, maybe it was hiding a bit when they hit it with the toxic treatments, only to come back stronger and smarter than before, that damn disease was ruthless, and ex-cuse my language, but I just have to say it, how is it possible for a disease to be so twisted, as if it enjoys causing pain? I can understand it when bacteria or vi-ruses attack, they're fighting for their own survival, in-fecting you so they can grow and multiply, but cancer? I just don't get it, it's like a twisted degeneration that only exists to cause suffering, like they say, we are our own worst enemies, thankfully, we started getting better news with the transplant, when they explained every-thing in detail, I didn't know whether to be happy or to run for the hills, what they were about to do to him was brutal, first, they were going to kill off all his remaining bone marrow with a chemotherapy treatment that made the previous ones seem like a walk in the park, they called it a "conditioning" treatment, but I mean, come on, how can they be so evasive with the truth? what it really did was prepare his body to receive his sister's stem cells, which would replace his marrow, but "condi-tioning"? it left his body so wrecked it might as well have been thrown in the trash! all the side effects he'd had before multiplied by four, they pumped the chemo into his veins through a catheter for six days, and he had nausea and diarrhea for three months afterward, can you imagine how awful it was right after the injection, if the effects lasted that long? it was pure poison, if it took three months to flush out, you can guess how he felt in the weeks that followed, on top of the usual side effects, he developed sores in his mouth that extended down his throat and deep into his esophagus, who knows how far they went, he couldn't even eat muffins anymore, and all his nutrition had to be administered intravenously, like a cow hooked up upside down to a milk machine, he'd carry around his feeding bag, pumping nutrients into him while he peed it all out just as fast, it was heartbreaking to see, thankfully, they gave him morphine, lots of it, at first, he asked for it timidly, afraid of getting addicted, but soon enough, he was requesting doses like a true junkie, one for the afternoon to pass the time, another at night to sleep, the morphine left him floating in a pleasant haze, he was much more likable, relaxed, and in that state, I could beat him at backgammon, chess, or whatever other game we played, he didn't care anymore, of course, that phase only lasted two or three weeks, afterward, he had to snap out of it, he couldn't stay in that dazed limbo forever, no matter how much he might have wanted to, I could already see they were planning to send him back home, and I wasn't too thrilled about it, first, they needed to make sure he was up and moving, eating again, and using the bathroom on his own, once that happened, it was back to me, Nurse-in-Chief, at home, I was trembling just thinking about how I'd manage everything, sure enough, once the transplant began to take hold, he started producing his own immune cells, he weaned off the morphine, and they sent him home to "enjoy" life again, that first week, he couldn't even walk from the sofa in the living room to the kitchen, and trust me, our apartment isn't big, with housing prices in Madrid the way they are, it's not like we're living in some grand estate with a "north wing" and a "south wing", we're talking maybe ten meters between rooms, if that, It's outrageous what they charge for a place here, whether you buy or rent, people say young folks have a tough time moving out on their own, but honestly, those of us who are a little less young are feeling the pinch too, the mortgage payments keep climbing, taxes are burning a hole in our pockets, the girls need money for this and that, and if they go abroad for their studies on an Erasmus program, we have to cover the rent, and it's not cheap in Northern Europe, let me tell you, it's ridiculously expensive, and even then, sometimes you can't find a decent place to live, no matter how much you're willing to pay, okay, I'm getting off-topic again, back to the point, when he tried to get up and walk, he'd get cramps, lose his balance, and stumble, I kept telling him, "be patient, you'll get there eventually" and once again, I had to reload my patience because I knew I'd need it, as for helping out around the house—forget it, he couldn't cook, clean, or do any shopping, absolutely nothing, and let me tell you, that annoyed me, because I'm not exactly rolling in free time, plus, we've always split household chores between us, say what you will about my husband, but he's always been good about pitching in around the house, and thank goodness for that, if not, I don't know if I'd have stayed with him all these years, I would've packed my bags and left, I don't even know where I would have gone, maybe traveling the world, hopping from one country to another, visiting the places I've always wanted to see, I would've stayed in hotels or cabins or wherever, I don't mind, I love talking to people, hearing their stories, learning where they're from and where they're headed, I just love the variety, new faces, new places, new monuments, I love it all, whether for its beauty or just for the fun of it, I could sit at a café and watch people pass by, or get on a bus and travel with the locals, that always entertains me, some places still have people boarding buses with chickens, headed straight to the cooking pot later, It makes you feel close to life itself, but, as fate would have it, I got what I got, so, instead of grand adventures, my travels were vacations with the family, working harder than if I'd stayed home, always making sure the bags were packed right, that no one forgot anything, cleaning up the messes we left behind, talk about anything but relaxing, the only time I get some peace is when they leave me alone on the beach with a book, which is what I love most, give me some time to myself, let me read for a bit, have a chat with a friend, that's all I ask, but back to where we were, little by little, he kept getting better, slowly but surely, one day, he managed to leave the house and walk all the way to the bakery, he'd sit down to rest for a while before heading back home, always with me by his side, he didn't dare go out alone, later, he worked up to walking a few blocks, always looking for benches to sit on when he got tired, eventually, we even managed to take walks together, which at least gave him some exercise and got us both out of the house, he started helping around the house a little more, but he still had those chimera-induced bouts of vomiting every few days, he started looking more like a normal person, for about three months, we were going to the hospital twice a week, they'd draw blood and discuss the results with the doctor, then we'd stop by the pharmacy to pick up a bunch of pills and head home to keep up with his recovery, the important thing was avoiding any complications, lung infections, skin rashes, rejection of the transplant, he did have some uncomfortable reactions, but nothing serious, at the end of that period, they ran a whole bunch of medical tests to see how he was holding up, they checked everything, his heart, liver, lungs, kidneys, and more, it turns out he wasn't as low-quality as I thought, and all the tests came back with good results, well, we left that phase behind and moved on to the next one, one thing they did was what they called the "chimerism test", they took his blood and analyzed the chromosomes to see how much was still his and how much was from his sister, the donor, three months in, he still had a bit of his own left, but they repeated the test every month, and soon enough, my sister-in-law took over completely, I was sure of that, though she's unstoppable, full of energy, so now I had a husband who was half man, half woman, it could've been worse! surely something good must rub off on him from us women! but this whole "half woman" thing has him obsessed, he keeps saying he doesn't understand how his marrow and blood could change, where did his original blood go? he says he gets how a kidney works since you can see how it gets flushed out, but what about the brain? how do you drain out every little vein and replace it with new blood without losing oxygen, which would supposedly kill the neurons? I tell him, "you don't understand it, and neither does anyone else, stop asking the doctor about it like you're trying to get a master's degree in medicine, it happens, that's all, you just have to believe it and hope for the best, no need to overthink it, look at pregnancy, that's a mystery! do we women overthink it or try to write a PhD thesis every time we're about to have a baby? no! we just have it, and that's it, we've got enough on our hands with the baby afterward without driving ourselves crazy with questions no one can answer, nature is wise, so the best thing you can do is trust it," and honestly, the doctors who treated him were very wise too, whenever I think about what they did to him and everything we went through, I'm just amazed, I'd rather get pregnant four more times than go through all that again, I don't tell him that, though, he'd get all cocky and macho about it, for all his talk about being "half woman," when his "manly side" comes out, it's just the same as ever! let's see if his feminine side shines through a little more, at least I'd be living with my best friend! after that whole first phase, I don't even know what to call it anymore, because they called it the first phase, but to me, it felt more like we were on the third, the latest thing was starting his vaccination schedule, they're like babies who lose their immune memory of all the vaccines they got as kids, so they have to get everything again: tetanus, diphtheria, whooping cough, polio, hepatitis, meningitis, herpes... you name it, all spaced out in monthly shots over eight months, they're going to turn him into a pincushion! But, as bad as it sounds, it's really nothing, he barely feels it, maybe a little discomfort after one of the vaccines, but nothing a painkiller and a good nap won't fix, and he has really developed his skill in good naps! he was already showing signs of being a great napper before the illness, but now he sleeps like a log after lunch, sometimes for more than two hours, the doctors say that's a good thing, that it helps him recover, so now I have to congratulate him for being such a good convalescent, well, fine, I'll congratulate him—it's no big deal, he spends all day at home, lazing around and claiming he's writing a novel, a novel, he says! When it's more like a jumble of nonsense, I don't even know if it's a novel or just another one of his chimeras, as he likes to call them, and trust me, my husband reads a lot, but writing? not so much, sure, he can write those scientific things that no one understands, but that doesn't count, no one reads those except with one eye closed, and you can write them with one hand tied behind your back, but writing a real novel, with well-developed characters, a mysterious plot, a love scene? he has no clue, writing takes practice, study, and preparation, with practice comes the skill and know-how, you don't just sit down and boom, out comes a novel like a hen laying an egg, you have to work for it, and to be fair, my husband puts in the hours, he spends all day in his study, sitting at his desk, typing away and reading, totally focused, maybe he's writing one of those well-researched historical novels that entertain while also teaching you something, those kinds of books people love, they take a lot of work, though, you have to gather tons of information, go to the archives, study up, but I don't think my husband is writing one of those, he's more of the "write whatever comes to mind" type, like anyone cares what he thinks, I believe he's just sitting there, all focused and dedicated, so no one bothers him and he can stay in his little world, I get it, honestly, he's been through hell in the hospital, tortured with all the treatments they gave him, now they've given him time to recover, so of course, he's going to rest and do what he wants, you can't expect much more from him, if he wants to sleep a lot or write, or if others want to paint, well, thank goodness he didn't turn into an artist!

that would've been the end of me, a messy easel getting in the way, oils scattered everywhere, the smell of turpentine, which I can't stand, and the delusions of grandeur every time he showed off his paintings, nope, it's better that he took up writing, if it's helping him recover, all the better, like I said, the important thing is that the transplant has taken root, and the hardest part is behind us, there's still a long way to go before he's fully recovered, but we'll get there, I've already prepared myself for it, plus, now that he's in charge of taking care of the house, I'm thrilled, it's freed me from all the burdens I've carried since this whole mess started, Nurse-in-Chief can retire and just give orders, as it should be, and for that, I'm grateful, it's allowed me to focus on my own things, which I'd had to abandon, but what I can't stand is that now he's coming at me with all this stuff about kindness and how love is the most important thing, it drives me crazy, seriously, my dear child, when have you ever done anyone any harm? what you need to do is snap out of it and stop giving us sermons like you've come back from the dead, you've got two days left, so make the most of them, carpe diem, and let's keep moving forward! he's becoming unbearable, talking about being a chimera, how well the nurses treat him, solving the Israel–Palestine conflict, Cervantes, Cernuda... but the worst is that now he's dead set on making a donation to cancer research, a monetary donation, no less, well, give the money to me! I could really use it, we've been stuck at home for so long, no movies, no restaurants, no trips, sex has become something we only see in films, let's get back to enjoying life and stop moralizing to everyone, it's unbearable! what we need are some good trips, we should visit every island in the

Mediterranean, once we've seen them all, we'll start with the Nordic countries, first Iceland, which everyone says is amazing with its volcanoes, hot springs, mountains, and incredible landscapes, we could travel around in a caravan, stopping wherever we like, staying warm inside while there's a blizzard outside, with icicles crashing down, we could head to the other Nordic countries when we get tired of Iceland: Norway, Sweden, Finland, I've already been to Denmark, so we can skip that, but I've never visited the other three, and I've been dying to go, but let's not go in the winter, I'm not that brave! just enough chill to snuggle up, but we'll wait until our summer starts and head north to escape the heat, springtime up there is perfect; you can enjoy it without melting like in Madrid, it's like you're postponing the worst of the summer swelter, and that's no small thing, the heat in big cities just wipes me out, in the countryside, it's different; there's always a breeze or some shade under a tree or by a fountain, but in the city, with the asphalt on fire it's unbearable! the idea of the fjords sounds so tempting, those breathtaking landscapes! no joke, they're so stunning you feel like you could fall backward just looking at them, although, maybe "falling" isn't the best expression, those cliffs are massive, and that's what makes it so beautiful, you can see them clearly on TV series with those aerial shots, zooming in and descending, it takes your breath away, and it's always sunny on those shows! I don't know how they do it, but it looks like the sun's always shining, they must take years to film or maybe they just rush out the moment the sun comes out to shoot outdoors, with days so long up there, they can shoot a whole series in just a few sunny days, that's one of the places I'd actually consider taking a cruise because, in the Mediterranean, no way! it's way too crowded, and they only let you see tourist traps, I know how those things work in my Andalusia, they herd you around the main sights, which are always surrounded by souvenir shops just to make you spend your money, then, once you've emptied your pockets, back on the cruise ship you go, but entering the fjords by boat must be worth it, feeling tiny amidst those towering cliffs, all green with huge pine trees clinging to the slopes right down to the water, just like the Vikings did, that's something I'd love, and with the evening chill setting in, I'd want him to hold me tight, with that soft, dim light that's so romantic, feeling his body close to mine, and for once, we'd leave behind all the illness, cancer, and cheap philosophy, we'd just get lost in the moment, in the sensations, in our feelings, like when we were young, feeling the warmth of the other person's body next to mine, appreciating his smell, his breath, listening to the sounds of life in him, I'd touch each of his lean muscles with my hands, telling him, "I'm here, I've been with you through all of this, carrying the weight of it all" and he'd say to me, "I know, and I love you, I always will, not just because you've stayed with me throughout this illness, but because I can't imagine life without you, I've always known you do whatever you want, but you're still my girl, my partner, and we'll be together until the end of the world."

VIII

Epilogue

The very act of writing this novel has helped me come to terms with my recent fate as a chimera. I am not some horrifying monster, though I still carry a bit of the mysterious and inexplicable within me. I tend to see myself as a new body I've been loaned in order to enjoy a few more years of life. I feel there must be a reason for my rebirth in this organism, a combination of two different somas, and if there isn't, I get the sense that dedicating my life to creating one is a worthwhile way to spend my time.

There are plenty of arguments to support my quest, as many circumstances had to come together for me to get this renewed opportunity. Had I suffered this illness twenty years ago, I most likely wouldn't have survived and would already be food for worms. Not that I fear becoming part of the earth's organic matter cycle, but it's clear the likely outcome would have been a circle of mushrooms rather than a novel.

By chance, my leukemia was detected in a routine blood test at the end of June. Had it not been for that, I would have finished the academic year in July and gone on vacation near the ocean, a trickster balm that soothes all ills. I don't know if I would have made it to the end of summer, but had I done so, I would have likely returned in September with a more advanced, uncontrollable disease.

The blood test was done at the hospital that corresponds to my area through the public healthcare system, the same one where I was urgently admitted and underwent treatments, from the initial rounds to the transplant. By chance, it happens to be one of the best hematology teams in Spain. Specialists in the disease I was afflicted with provided me with the necessary care swiftly and efficiently. As a university professor and civil servant, I get to choose at the start of every year—during the month of January—whether to be covered by private medical insurance or the public system. For over a decade, I had been with a private insurance provider because it offered some conveniences for minor day-to-day health issues. However, after the COVID-19 pandemic, I decided to switch back to public healthcare that January as recognition for the vital work done by the public health service in such difficult times. If I had stayed with the private provider, the blood test and leukemia treatment would have probably taken place in a private clinic, perhaps well-attended but surely handled by a less specialized medical team than the one I was fortunate to have under public healthcare.

Other coincidences followed. Only minor complications arose—like infections or rejections—throughout the process of chemotherapy and transplant, which, after months in an oncology ward and hearing all the things that could go wrong, was truly fortunate. The full compatibility of my younger sister's marrow with mine was within the usual probability range, as being one of five siblings it was expected that at least one of them would be a match. In any case, having the option of a close family member as a donor, who was also fully willing to assist, sped up the process and made my recovery smoother since graft-versus-host rejection issues were minimal and manageable.

It's a series of coincidences, surely I could find more if I looked closely, that all added up to the fact that it wasn't yet my time to leave this world. Without underestimating chance, which governs the world in apparent absurdity, it feels almost inevitable to try to make sense of this second opportunity that fate has granted me. Where it has led me, I've already said—to the conviction that I must contribute my small grain of sand to a vital humanism that helps revalue our existence. How I will go about it still needs explaining.

If there was one youthful dream I set aside, out of fear or shame, it was the desire to dedicate myself to literature. Reading has always been my great passion, expressing feelings and thoughts through words has always been my unfinished task. Perhaps that's why, faced with the difficult health circumstances I've had to endure, my reaction was to jot down what was running through my head in a notebook and then write to revel in what I had noted. That's where this novel comes from—after many years on hold, it has taken shape thanks to the illness I suffered.

I hope you won't be angry with me for being pretentious and daring to end with a monologue akin to Molly Bloom's from Ulysses. It's an homage to one of my favorite novels, a great literary chimera, timeless, that guided the 20th century and still hovers over the present.

It is also dedicated to the support and love I received throughout this time from my wife, who was always by my side in the toughest moments. Whether for Joyce, for Cervantes, or for Homer, for boldness, for the freedom to write whatever one pleases—this is for them all. For literature as a wonderful tool of creation that helps us imagine an existence, so we can understand and come to terms with the harsh reality that confronts us.

For all of them, and for everything said, I sign off this wild chimera toasting with a glass of good wine and an open mind.

Madrid, January 2025

Notes

[1] Paul Diel (1952). Published in 1980 as *Symbolism in Greek Mythology: Human Desire and its Transformations* (V. Stuart, M. Stuart & R. Folkman, Trans.). Shambhala. Boulder, CO, USA.

[2] Robert Graves (1955). The Greek Myths. Penguin, London. UK.

[3] Luis Cernuda (1962). Published in 2009 as *Desolation of the Chimera*. White Pine Press. Buffalo, NY, USA.

[4] Gerard de Nerval.(1854). Published in 2023 as *Sylvie & The Chimeras*. Sunny Lou Publishing Company, Portland, OR, USA.

[5] Reference to a verse from *Desolation of the Chimera* by Cernuda (Note 3).

[6] Beryl Markham (1942). *West with the night*. Open Road Media. New York, NY,. USA.

[7] Global Observatory on Donation and Transplantation. https://www.transplant-observatory.org. Verified January 2025.

[8] Organización Nacional de trasplantes. https://www.ont.es. Verified January 2025.

[9] Worldwide Network for Blood & Marrow Transplantation. https://www.wbmt.org. Verified January 2025.

[10] Paul Craddock. (2021). *Spare Parts. The Story of Medicine Through the History of Transplant Surgery*. St. Martin Press, NY, USA.

[11] Josep Carreras Foundation against leukemia. https://fcarreras.org. Verified January 2025. These survival rates improve every year, so they are expected to be higher with time.

Acknowledgments

My deepest gratitude to Cécile Thibaud and Andrés Fernández Rubio, both journalists and writers, who were the first readers of the novel. They gave me great advice to refine the initial manuscript and encouraged me to continue until I finished it.

Judit Sáenz-Badillos and Isabella Athanassiou did an excellent job with the corrections and provided great style suggestions—thank you. Judit's opinion as a physician helped me to avoid mistakes in medical terms. I also appreciate the work of the editor Isabel Montes; without her, the publication of this book would not have been possible.

Thanks to Inés and Ana for reading the novel and sharing their opinions. Another way of helping their father, which adds to all the love I received during my illness.

Thanks also to my brothers and sisters, who have been supportive whenever needed.

Thank you for reading new literary talent.
I hope you enjoyed the read.

Feel free to visit our Bookstore
https://angelsfortune.com/

Follow us on our social networks to stay informed.

Isabel Montes
Writer and founding publisher of
Angels Fortune Publishing Group

www.ingramcontent.com/pod-product-compliance
Lightning Source LLC
Chambersburg PA
CBHW020921160726
47993CB00005B/2066